THE LYNCHING
OF A PASTOR

The Lynching
of a Pastor

Chester Reddrick

To order additional copies of this book, contact:
Xlibris Corporation
1-888-795-4274
www.Xlibris.com
Orders@Xlibris.com
21328

CONTENTS

Dedicated to my Grandparents, my Mother and Father,
Chet, Martin, Maliek, my Sisters and Brothers,

A Dear Cousin, Betty Foy Scavella, a little village called
Leland, where I was raised and loved,

and all of The Village Family.

FOREWORD

This is a true story of a successful pastor who was slandered by his wife and church officers. Unable to obtain an investigation by the church or a trial by the civil court that would have cleared his name, this man's reputation was lynched, his pastorate destroyed, his income and marriage of thirty years lost.

Left homeless and penniless, it was a vision from God, the worshiping of God, and some devoted friends and former church members that were the source of his enduring strength, despite the devil's attempt to destroy God's purpose for his life.

ACKNOWLEDGMENTS

When this book was first published, I didn't aggressively promote it for two reasons; like a thief, lingering grief continued to steal my confidence and the recognition that the book needed further editing. But in time, like the Biblical Joseph, God sent me someone who made me forget my pain. Not only has Liz become the sugar in my lemonade, but she also just happens to have editing skills. It was her editing work and her encouragement, as well as a positive comment by her daughter after reading the book, that ignited my passion to now aggressively promote the book.

To Liz I owe a great deal of thanks.

INTRODUCTION

Lynching usually means the killing, generally by hanging, of a person by a mob in defiance of law and order. The victim does not have a chance to defend himself. The mob simply assumes him guilty, whether or not he has had a trial. Lynch mobs not only promote disrespect for law, order, and basic human rights but also encourage mass brutality.

The term lynching probably originated with Charles Lynch, a planter who lived in Virginia during the 1700's. Lynch and his neighbors took the law into their own hands and punished Tories (British sympathizers) and others who plundered their property. The term came to be applied to physical punishment such as whipping and tarring and feathering. In pioneer communities on the far western frontier, many lynch mobs punished persons for horse stealing, highway robbery, or murder. Lynching began to take the form of hangings.

During this period, people took the law into their own hands because there was no duly established legal authority. With the establishment of law and order throughout the United States, lynch mobs began to act in opposition to the law, instead of supporting it.

Before 1890, most lynching victims were white. Since then, most lynchings have occurred in the South, and the victims have usually been Negroes. About 4,752 lynchings occurred between 1882 and 1968, including 1,307 whites and 3,445 Negroes. The peak year for these killings was 1892, with 230 victims. No recorded

lynchings have taken place since 1968. New England
is the only section of the United States in which no
lynchings have ever occurred. (Marvin E. Wolfgang, The
World Book Encyclopedia, l Volume 12, 467)

While I was not physically lynched, my reputation and character
were. That the leaders of the lynching party were deacons and
trustees, and that the lynching mob itself was church members
have implications, I think, for all of us who love God and His
kingdom.

CHAPTER 1

The False Allegation

According to Edward Hiscox,

> Great caution should be exercised, even in giving heed to unfavorable reports against a minister of the gospel. Christ's anointed ones should not be touched with unholy hands. The apostle wisely decreed that, 'against an elder, receive not an accusation except at the mouth of two or three witnesses' (First Timothy 5:19). Charges which implicate their moral or ministerial character should not be entertained only on very strong evidence. Their position is a very delicate one. Called by professional duties into almost all sorts of company, and placed in well-nigh all kinds of positions, evil minded persons can, if disposed excite suspicions against them on the most trivial occasions. (Edward T. Hiscox, Principles and Practices for Baptist Churches, pp-206-207)

That is what happened to me.

My tragedy began on Friday December 7, 2001 when I overheard my wife, Loraine, talking on the phone to our grandson's mother. She was asking Nakia to bring him over that afternoon to spend the weekend and help her put up Christmas decorations. When she left for work that morning she didn't say what time she would be home or what time she was expecting the child to be brought over. I was happy and looking forward to seeing him. We both wished that the circumstance of his birth had been different—that is born in a traditional family where his mother and father were married. But our grandchild had nothing to do with that. Although I was hurt at first I soon got over it and this precious child had become the source of much joy in my life. My wife however, never seemed to fully accept it. Although she was good to him, she never unconditionally embraced him with all her heart. It causes me pain and embarrassment to admit this, but she despised his mother. In her opinion, she was just not good enough for her son. In fact, she felt that she was responsible for corrupting our son. But on the phone that morning she was very cordial and polite. I was happy about that because I knew that was good for our grandson. An environment of love is the best gift that one can give a child. I wanted him to have all the love and validation I tried to give to my own children. Since his father was not able to provide for him yet, we both took on the role of surrogate parents.

For several days I had been infected with a severe sinus infection. I was taking antibiotics and was left tired and weak but by that Friday I was beginning to feel much better. Much of that morning I spent working in the house cleaning, in anticipation of the Christmas holidays. Around 3:00 p.m., I lay down in order to be well rested when our grandson came over later that afternoon. At exactly 4 p.m., the phone rang. I knew it was 4 p.m. because when it rang, I looked at the clock on the nightstand. I started not to answer it because I had just begun to relax. But as a minister I never know when someone may need to speak to me, so I answered. It was our grandson's mother.

She said, "Mr. Reddrick, is Mrs. Reddrick home yet?" I said no, and then I went on to tell her that I thought she would be home in about an hour or an hour and a half. It was just a guess but because this was an arrangement made between the two of them and since school was out at 2:30 I just naturally assumed that she would definitely be home at least by then if not earlier.

She said, "Okay, thank you."

I hung the phone up and remained in bed trying to rest. But it was then that I did wonder why Mrs. Reddrick didn't tell her what time she would be home. Some time later, and I am not certain how much later, maybe an hour or an hour and a half, the doorbell rang. I got up and went to the door. It was our grandson and his mother. He was grinning from ear-to-ear. I naturally told them to come on in. After normal greetings to both of them, I suggested to him that we take the dog out. My grandson was just five years old at the time and we lived right in front of a busy road, so I was not about to let him take the dog out by himself. When we walked out the door his mother came along. When we came back in the house, he went upstairs to the bathroom. His mother went in the den to watch the television and I went in the kitchen and washed a few dirty dishes. While there, I called my wife on her cell phone to tell her that our grandson and Nakia had arrived, but her phone was off. Since he did not immediately come down from the bathroom, his mother went up to check on him and afterwards came back into the den to watch television. A few minutes later the child came down and joined his mother in the den where they both sat watching the television. It was then that I noticed that I had not heard the bathroom commode flush. I went upstairs to check and sure enough, like most young children, he did not flush it. I flushed it and just as I suspected, it was stopped up.

I went downstairs in the garage and got a plunger, a bucket and the mop. I went back upstairs and unstopped it, washed out the commode, and mopped the floor. I then took the dirty rugs, the bucket and the mop back downstairs in the garage where the washing machine was also located. While there I decided to put a load of dirty clothes in the washer including those rugs from the bathroom. As I did that, my wife came home. She entered the house through the garage where she found me putting clothes in the washer. I remember her looking at me rather strangely, but at the time, I didn't know why. I spoke as she walked past me, entering the den where our grandson and his mother were still sitting watching television. She greeted them warmly and they greeted her warmly in return, although, our grandson appeared to be typically shy. Before she sat down, my wife went upstairs, and put down, I believe her book bags, and then rejoined our grandson and his mother in the den.

I was happy that she was finally home and was now entertaining them. Feeling a little exhausted, I then went upstairs and stretched out on the bed. I rested in anticipation of playing with my energetic grandson when his mother left. At the time, little did I know that this was the beginning of a horror story that would change all of our lives forever.

Our grandson spent the weekend and had a wonderful time. But Loraine didn't put up Christmas decorations as she had planned. I also noticed that she spent a lot of time with him. I was happy about that because normally I had been the primary babysitter. Something else was a little strange but not terribly so. Loraine did not go to church with me that Sunday morning, and seemed depressed, and as I think about it now, she was angry. I had seen these moods many times before and was certain that it would pass as they had always done. After a couple of days of the cold shoulder treatment, I asked her what was wrong? The response was an icy cold silence. When she came home that Tuesday evening I was concerned that there was no change in her disposition and felt that it was now time to find out what was going on. So I asked again, but this time with much more vigor, "What's wrong with you?"

In an angry and defiant tone her response was, "You slept with that girl!" At first I couldn't believe what I had heard, but the certainty in her tone of voice, coupled with the ferociousness of her anger was a clear and undeniable indication to me that my wife was dead serious.

I met Loraine when she was eighteen years old. We were both in college. I fell in love with her at first sight. She was my Queen of Sheba. She was my Cleopatra. After thirty years of marriage, to me this woman was still the apple of my eyes. Although she was never totally committed to the goals and values that possessed me, she was still supportive of my ministry, and I always supported her in her profession. She had been an elementary school teacher for over thirty years and a very good one at that. She loved her work but like some older teachers she was getting fed up with all the new changes. She was beginning to look forward to retirement.

At this same time there was another crisis that visited the Reddrick household. It involved our youngest son. He appeared to be a perfect child. He got into no trouble in his teenage years. He did not go through the stages of rebellion that is so common with children of his age. He was on the high school football team. He played the organ at church. He sang in the choir, and he went off to college as was expected. But after three years there, he got connected with the wrong group of people and went astray. The trouble he got into involved money and when we found out about it, he was already in court. Our family grief was almost unbearable. What would our friends think? What would the church members think? I read with new interest the story of Hosea and his family, and I had heard of other ministers' children who had fallen from grace, but never thought it could happen to me. And if that was not a heavy enough burden, now this! I began to question God.

When I answered my wife, her response was as if I'd poured gasoline on a burning fire. She exploded to a new level of anger. I'd never seen this character. The more I denied it the worse she became. Days went by and then another Sunday, but no change. People at church began to ask, "Where is Mrs. Reddrick?"

I told them that she was at home and that she was not feeling well. With her anger and viciousness growing worse, helplessness and fear began to swallow me. Then one night in a verbal rage she made a comment that justified my feelings of impotence and fear. She said, "I'm going to tell our grandson's father and the deacons at the church what you did!" By now I'd come to acknowledge to myself that this was bigger than me. I prayed and asked God to show me the meaning of all this. I was in a territory that I'd never been before. All my wisdom and knowledge was of no help. Most of my life had been spent in helping other people. I was a preacher, a man of God and my wife was the first lady of the church. Who could I go to and tell that my wife believed that I had slept with our grandson's mother in our home with our grandson present? A few days before Christmas, our oldest son, our grandson's father, called me. He was in the navy and was doing well. He was by then happily married to a wonderful young lady. Economically, he was able to fulfill his responsibility to his son whom he loved very much. He was planning to complete his college degree and for that I was very happy.

He said, "Daddy, what's wrong with Mama?"

I responded, "What do you mean?"

He said, "Mama sounds like she's losing it; she said she believes you slept with Nakia."

Then he said, "Daddy I know you, I don't believe one word of it." "This thing is worrying me," he said. "I need to talk to somebody."

After briefing him on what had taken place in the home over the past three weeks, we both agreed that his grandmother, Loraine's mother, would be the ideal person to talk to now. It was our hope that she would use her considerable influence with her daughter, and help us figure out what was wrong with her. Fortunately for me, neither of our sons believed this tragic story

Now I realized that she'd told this diabolical tale to someone else, but it was still in the family. My hope now rested in her mother, our children, and her sisters and brothers. Nevertheless, this thought now occurred to me, had she really said anything to the deacons? I felt certain that if she had, they would have mentioned it to me. My worse fear was the embarrassment of it all.

On Christmas day my wife went home to her mother as she had done for the past thirty years. Sometimes I would go, and sometimes I would stay at home. But that year I had nothing to rejoice about. My life was like a ship struggling to stay afloat in a violent storm. For the first time in my life, I spent Christmas day in bed surrounded with grief, stress, mourning, and fear. They all kept me company that day.

When the holiday was over, my wife came back home but she was still the same. I decided then that we needed some professional help. My wife exemplified symptoms that suggested that something dramatic had happened to her. She totally believed this story. She cried when she told it. She said the child told her that his granddaddy and mama were in the bedroom. She was in emotional torment and pain. The hope that I had in her mother did not bear fruit. She believed her daughter, and said to me, that all men were like that, and that the best thing for me to do was to admit it; confess to God, and go get another Baptist church.

On the first day of the new year, I finally heard from God. He spoke to me in a vision. In this dream, I was eating Chinese food. When I finished eating the food, I noticed there was a little box on the plate about the size of a matchbox. I opened it but there was nothing inside but some white paper that looked like the kind of paper that one might find in pill bottles to keep pills fresh. I removed that paper and a little black snake just started moving. It jumped out of the box and landed on the floor growing right before my eyes. Something told me to get up and find something to kill it before it killed me. I ran down stairs in the garage got a pick ax, and ran back upstairs: It now was a giant snake. I struck it in the head with the sharp end of the pick ax, and I watched it die. I felt jubilant afterwards. Something said to me, "This thing that is coming against you is big enough to kill you, but it won't kill you now because you've killed it." I was convinced that this was a sign from God that I would survive this tribulation.

On the first Sunday of the new year I saw some bad omens in the church. The chairman of the deacon board held his head down and did not respond to my sermon; another deacon did not take communion; and another one left church early under the pretext of taking his wife to the hospital. It was only later that I really found out the reasons for those actions. The congregation, however, responded to my sermon as usual. In fact, one young man rededicated his life to God that Sunday. I asked the church to pray for my son and my family and as much as I tried to ignore it, I felt a shift in the wind coming out of the deacon's corner and it was cold.

A few days later, actually that Tuesday evening, I had an appointment to see a counselor and later that evening I would have my first deacon board meeting of the new year. Although, I was heavily burdened by personal twin crises, I took consolation from the vision and from the fact that I was leading the congregation in the building of a new sanctuary, something that would have been thought impossible a few years ago. I had been there now 14 years. What a miracle!

For the first time in my life I had to talk to someone about my family. It was hard for me to do. I felt a sense of inadequacy. I felt embarrassed and humiliated. Yet I knew I needed some professional help. When the counselor finally started the session, I started thinking about the many times I had sat down with people in an effort to help them. Now the roles were reversed. When I finished telling the counselor the story, the look on her face alarmed me. She said, "Have you told the deacons?" I said, not yet. Then she said this, "This thing is like an octopus." She was very caring and compassionate, and wanted to talk to my wife in a private session and then to both of us together. I was totally in agreement with that and would have been willing to do anything that she suggested. I was desperate. When I left there I went right to the church for the deacon board meeting that I had called. When I walked in the room, they were all there. But something else was there too. The atmosphere was poison. The fumes of condemnation engulfed me. Right away I realized that sympathy was not there; that empathy was not there; that compassion was not there. Condemnation was the only spirit present. Since I was late, I set aside the normal routine. After prayer, I apologized for being late and opened the discussion by asking them if there was anything that they wanted to bring to my attention. The chairman spoke up and said, "Yes Pastor, there is something, we had hoped that you would have told us, but you didn't. Your wife came to me and told me that she came home and caught you in the bed with your grandson's mother."

Not certain if I really heard him and wondering if he had maybe made a mistake. I said, "What!"

He said, "Yes, those are her very words. She said she came home and caught you in bed with your grandson's mother."

Nothing I said mattered. These men that I had known, worked with and struggled with for fourteen years to make the church a better church were now transformed before my very eyes, it seemed. That same spirit that possessed my wife was now possessing them. I examined each face looking for some support: I found none. Another one even spoke up and said, "That's right, Reverend Reddrick; she told me the same thing."

Then I referred to the scripture, where it said no charges should be entertained against an elder except there be two or three witnesses. The chairman said, "That don't apply in this case."

Then another one said angrily, "You need to step down from the pulpit until we find out the truth."

In response to that I said, "If you do something like that without following the rules of the church and the bylaws, I'll take every penny I've got and sue you."

Another one said, "Well, let us bring Mrs. Reddrick in here and talk to her and let us see who's telling the truth."

Again I referred to the rules and the church procedures for handling such matters. But they didn't seem to be interested in those.

The chairman spoke again and said, "We got to do something about this thing before it gets all over the church."

I replied, "I'll go before the church and explain to the church the truth of the matter. I've always told these people the truth; I have nothing to hide here."

They objected to that. We concluded the meeting with the agreement that I would go to each department or auxiliary of the church and tell the members the situation.

On the way home after the meeting, I started mentally going over every detail of the encounter; the men's anger; the allegation that my wife had said that she caught me in bed with our grandson's mother; the dismissal of any adherence to scripture, the church bylaws; or any rules of common courtesy. And there was the other comment made by the chairman and the way he said it, "We got to hold onto what we got here." By his tone and demeanor, I knew that "holding on to what we got here" did not include me. I was amazed that the men were totally dismissing all of my accomplishments and were now virtually claiming them as their own. There was this other comment made by one of them, it was a slip of the tongue, but I heard enough of it to realize that they had already had a secret meeting prior to meeting with me. And of course, this question, *Did my wife tell them that she came home and caught me in the bed with my grandson's mother?*

I would soon find out. But I knew I had to be careful in the way I asked her. She was still irrational and volatile. I decided that the best way to confront her with this question was to be very calm and to conceal from her my fears, pain, anger, and all of my frustrations. I did not want to add fuel to her burning rage, which had not subsided since it started in early December.

At approximately ten o'clock that night, I went to the bedroom. She was in bed but not asleep yet. She looked tired, stressed, and estranged. However, she was calm. It felt a temporary lull in what had been an on-going storm. I gently asked, "Did you tell the deacons that you came home and caught me in bed with Nakia?" She looked up at me with her eyes more focused on me now and said, "No. You know I wouldn't tell a lie on you. You were in the garage when I came home."

I said, "I know, I just want to know did you tell anyone that." Again, she reiterated what she had already said and then asked me why I was asking her that. I told her that I had a deacon's meeting earlier that evening and that two of the deacons told me in the meeting that this is what she had said. She vehemently denied that she told either one of them that. She said that she did talk to them as she said she would, but she continued to deny their retelling. I kept thinking to myself even if she told them that, why aren't they abiding by the church bylaws, the Bible, the Hiscox Guide, or the Robert's Rules of Order, all of which have the proper procedure for handling such a matter. I questioned who was bringing the charge against me? Something kept saying over and over again, *They are using this situation to destroy you and your ministry here at this church. The chairman of the board and some of his cohorts are the leaders of it; they are refusing to abide by the rules because they fear that even with the slanderous lie the majority of the members would not vote to oust you in a proper vote.*

Now the vision that I'd had took on even greater meaning for me. I knew now without any doubt that I was in serious trouble. When this thing first started, the embarrassment of it all was my major concern and of course what was wrong with my wife. Now this accusation had escalated into a full-scale scandal and I was in a fight for my life. I felt like an animal when suddenly trapped. I felt the pain of betrayal. I trusted one of those deacons with my life. There was no question now that this tragedy had moved from the confines of the family circle into the congregation. That fact now and the new version of events momentarily reunited my wife and me. We embraced and reconfirmed our love for each other. But as the night grew longer my eyes became a faucet of running water. My grief was uncontrollable. How could church people, how could church deacons, men who are supposed to be full of the Holy Spirit do this to another human being? That Friday evening I met with one of the church auxiliaries as we had agreed to in the deacons' meeting. But unsurprising to me the word was already out. When I told them the true story, again my grief—no matter how hard I struggled to contain it—overwhelmed me. What I remembered most about the meeting was how different it was from the deacons' meeting. The people there were sympathetic, kind, and compassionate. And after prayer, they embraced me and spoke heartfelt words of encouragement, words that comforted my troubled soul.

CHAPTER 2

Kicked Out Of The Church

When I went to the church Sunday morning I was emotionally and spiritually wounded. In spite of all that had occurred during the week, I was still not prepared for or aware of what was awaiting me there. The auxiliary meeting had gone well on Friday and I would continue meeting with them until I met with all of them. After all, that was the decision arrived at in the contentious board meeting. So I had no reason to expect anything out of the ordinary on Sunday morning.

However, when I got up to review the Sunday school lesson, the deacons surrounded me. The chairman said angrily, "We want to see you in the study."

I refused to go. I decided right there on the spot that I was not going to be a willing participant in my own lynching. I said to the members there, "This rumor that is circulating here about me is absolutely false." Then I reminded them of the facts in the church bylaws of the correct procedure for handling such a matter, but that procedure was not being followed. Some spoke up in agreement, but some looked on in silence. I could tell by the looks on the faces of everyone there that they all had heard this lie. I thought to myself, these deacons have done a good job. But I wouldn't move and they wouldn't move. Then a lady spoke up with what I thought was a good idea.

She said "Reverend Reddrick, I love you and I love the deacons." Her husband was one of the deacons, and I always thought that she was a very good Christian. "Why don't you and the deacons go over into the other building, have prayer and resolve this matter without further disruption within the church?"

I agreed with that on the condition that they abide by it. The chairman balked and said, he wasn't going. I said to him, "I'm going to stand right here." The standoff continued until one of them said, "We'll go."

Inside the other building the chairman acted like a man possessed. One would have thought that we'd been opposing warlords engaged in a long protracted war. He pointed his finger at me and said tauntingly to the others, both deacons and trustees, "This man has been disrespecting me now for a long time."

I had no idea of what incidents of disrespect he was referring. I recalled not attending one of his Masonic events. I thought to myself, *Could that be it, a personal vendetta?*

In a non-provocative tone, the chairman of the trustee board spoke up and said, "Reverend Reddrick, we just want you to step down from the pulpit until this matter is investigated, that's all".

I said that only on one condition, that the bylaws are adhered to. A deacon responded, "No; no bylaws!"

I knew I was at a disadvantage. My wife, while admitting that she did not tell the deacons the story that had been circulating, nevertheless, believed with certainty that I slept with Nakia prior to her arrival home, and no amount of denial mattered to her. Because of her emotional state, she was very convincing to anyone who wanted to believe her story, and I had no evidence yet to disprove her claims. To make matters worse, I now would not even have the benefit of due process afforded to the accused inherent in the procedures outlined in the Hiscox Guide for Baptist churches that is referred to in the church bylaws.

In light of that, I then demanded that they put their request in writing. At that they agreed. They sent for the church clerk to type up the document; I felt that under the circumstances I'd won a victory. While waiting for the secretary to type up the agreement, in walked my wife. Surprised at her presence, I asked her why she was there. She said a member of the church had called her and told her that they would not allow me in the pulpit and that she came over to go before the congregation to tell them that she did not tell the deacons the story that they had told the members. The church clerk handed me a copy of the signed agreement. I requested from her a copy of the church bylaws. With both in hand, my wife and I decided to go home. The following is a copy of the document.

Mount Calvary Missionary Baptist Church
924 North Eighth Street
Wilmington, North Carolina 28401
January 13, 2002

Sunday, January 13, 2002

The Board of Deacons and Trustess met with the chairman of Deacons on Sunday January 13, 2002 at 11:00a.m.. The purpose of the meeting was to asked Reverend Chester H. Reddrick to sit down from the pulpit with pay until the accusation against him has been resolved.

A motion was made by Deacon Joseph Canty, Sr. and seconded by Deacon James Aiken

George Vereen, Chariman   *George Vereen*

John Green, Chairman Trustee Board   *John C. Green*

Kenneth Drakeford, Secretary of Board of Deacons
Kenneth Drakeford
Rena Lennon, Church Clerk
Rena Lennon

Reverend C. H. Reddrick
W. C. H. Reddrick W.

With no legal or human rights protection in the church now, and finding myself in the hands of unholy men, I felt that I had no choice but to seek an attorney. That was the number one item on my Monday morning's agenda. Finally, after obtaining a 4 p.m. appointment, I took with me the letter of agreement, a copy of the church bylaws, which had been approved by the church approximately ten years before the incident, and was one of the inclusions in the new member's booklet, which had been in existence for several years. I also took a book entitled, the Hiscox Guide for Baptist churches, which contains the principles, practices, and procedures that most Baptist churches try to adhere. After the consultation, he agreed to represent me.

That night a member of the church called and said, "Reverend Reddrick, I just want to know. Did any of the deacons have the common courtesy to call you and tell you that a meeting is being held at the church on Thursday night?"

I answered, "No, not yet."

I just assumed that the purpose of it was to explain to the congregation the terms of the agreement made on Sunday and to answer the questions that many of the members had pertaining to the accusation and the course of action that they'd taken. Nevertheless, I notified my attorney, and he sent this letter to the deacons and trustees, along with a copy of the proper procedure for the termination of a pastorate, according to the Hiscox Guide, which is also referred to in the bylaws.

Hall & Horne, L.L.P.
TRIAL ATTORNEYS
718 MARKET STREET
WILMINGTON, NORTH CAROLINA 28401

ALEXANDER M. HALL
ROSEANNA C. HORNE
JOHN F. GREEN II

TELEPHONE (910) 343-8433
FAX (910) 343-8165

January 15, 2002

Mr. Joseph Canty
Mr. William Nixon
Mr. Kenneth Drakeford
Mr. David Brown
Mr. James Aiken
Mr. William Brunson
Mr. George Veereen
Mr. John Green
Mr. Leroy Brown
Mr. Charles Dowe
Mr. Isaiah Thomas
Ms. Rosetta Geddie
Mr. Allen Drakeford

Re: Allegation of misconduct against Rev. Chester H. Reddrick

Gentlemen and Madam:

    This letter is addressed to you as members of the Board of Deacons and Trustee's Board of Mount Calvary Missionary Baptist Church. Please be advised that we have been asked to represent Rev. Reddrick, on the misconduct charge which has been made against him. We are presently in the process of conducting an investigation in this matter to determine whether or not these charges have any validity. Frankly, to date, we do not see anything which would even remotely be considered competent evidence of any misconduct such as been alleged against Rev. Reddrick.

    Until we have complete an investigation, which I assure you will be done very promptly, we ask that you take no further action regarding Rev. Reddrick's service at your church. We understand that there is a meeting being called, exactly the nature of which we do not know, for Thursday of this week. Under the circumstances we believe it wise that such meeting either not be held or if such a meeting is held that no adverse action be taken against Rev. Reddrick at that time.

    The publicity of this matter has apparently caused a discord within the church and it is apparent that it was not pursued with the deliberate and careful consideration that should have been given to the issue. I think it very important that you do not rush to any ill advised conclusion in this case without all of the facts.

    If a pastor is to be terminated, then the provisions of your by-laws regarding termination of a pastor must be complied with. Furthermore, I am enclosing herein for your consideration pages 65 through 69 of the Hiscox Guide for Baptist Churches, which I believe sets forth clearly the duties and obligations which are imposed after a charge of misconduct has been leveled against a pastor.

    Upon completion of the investigation, we would like to meet with you regarding this matter.

    With kind regards, I remain

                    Very truly yours,

                    John Felix Green, II

JFG/sf

cc: Rev. Chester H. Reddrick

Enclosure

throughout all Judea and Galilee and Samaria, and were edified; and walking in the fear of the Lord, and in the comfort of the Holy Ghost, were multiplied" (Acts 9:31).

NOTE 1.—In calling a man to the pastorate, the church should take deliberate care to know his record; what he has done elsewhere, and how he is esteemed and valued where he has previously lived and labored. It is a folly of which churches are often guilty—and for which they justly suffer—that on the credit of a few flashy or fascinating sermons, wholly ignorant of his private character and of his ministerial history, they call and settle a pastor. A man of deep Christian commitment, thoroughly in love with the word of God, is much to be preferred to the brilliant pulpiteer.

NOTE 2.—If a young man without a record is called to be ordained and begin his pastorate, his reputation for commitment, sound sense, and pulpit ability should be carefully considered and well understood. If he be of the right spirit and the right material, he will grow into larger usefulness through study, the endowment of the Spirit, and the prayers of the people.

NOTE 3.—In giving a *call*, the church usually appoints a meeting for that express purpose, notice being publicly given two Sundays in succession, the purpose of the meeting being distinctly stated in the notice, and a three-quarters vote of all present at such a meeting should be deemed essential to a call. Certainly no self-respecting man would accept a call on anything less than that. Such meeting should be managed with Christian sincerity, and the candidate should be informed exactly how the vote stands, and what the feeling toward him is, concealing nothing.

H. ACCUSED MINISTERS

One of the most grave and difficult cases of discipline which is likely to arise to vex and possibly to

divide a church is that of a minister who has lost
public confidence, and who, by unchristian or un-
ministerial conduct, is believed to be unfit to dis-
charge the functions of, or to remain in, the sacred
office.

Great caution should be exercised, even in giving
heed to unfavorable reports against a minister of the
gospel. The Apostle wisely decreed, "Against an
elder, receive not an accusation but before two or:
three witnesses" (1 Tim. 5:19). Charges which im-
plicate their moral or ministerial character should
not be entertained, except on very strong evidence.
Their position is a very delicate one. Called by professional duties into almost all sorts of company, and
placed in well-nigh all kinds of positions, they can
become the victims of suspicions aroused by evil-
minded persons against them on the most trivial
occasions. They themselves are bound to exercise
perpetual vigilance and care, while their reputation
and good character, on which their comfort and usefulness so much depend, should be sacredly guarded
and defended. But their sins should not be covered
when they deserve exposure, nor should they escape
discipline when they merit it.

Such cases are likely to be important and difficult, because:

First—Of the high position and wide influence of
a minister, and the fact that he stands before the
public as an example of godliness, a religious teacher
and leader of the people. If he proves himself an unworthy man, his case becomes more a reproach to
religion, and more an obstacle to the progress of

truth than if he were a private member of the church.

Second—A minister's character and good name must be held sacredly and dealt with tenderly, since they are his richest possessions. They must not be trifled with.

In dealing with such a case, therefore, unusual caution should be exercised; and there are few churches so strong, so wise, so well balanced and so self-contained that it would be prudent to proceed to extremities without in some way securing outside aid and advice, most likely through the association or the state convention. In many instances, with such guidance, deacons or other officers of the church can bring the matter to a satisfactory solution by private conference with the pastor.

In the most extreme situations, a council similar to an ordination council may be convened to review the case and make suitable recommendations. Such a council may suggest, after hearing both the accusations and the defense, some disciplinary action, or may vote that he has been wronged and should be cleared of all charges.

A council called to advise in matters relating to the trial of an accused minister can only be called by a church; and by that church of which such minister is a member. Having no ecclesiastical authority, it cannot be called to try, nor if he is found guilty, to depose a minister. Judicial acts belong to a church, and not to a council; nor can a church transfer its authority for the exercise of judicial functions to any other body. A council, in order to express an opinion and give advice, is asked to examine all the facts, consider all the circumstances, sift and weigh the e\`' dence on all sides, the accused having full oppo tunity to defend himself. In a modified, but not in a judicial sense, it may be called a trial of the accused, because it is a search for the merits of the case by an investigation of all the facts and a sifting of all the evidence.

The minister on whose case his church may call a council is not obliged, and cannot be compelled, to appear before such a council, or in any way submit his case to them. But it is his *right* to appear before them, have copies of all charges, hear all testimony, examine witnesses, and answer for himself, and usually it is better for him to take this course. It is better for one to meet all charges frankly, and all accusers face to face, than to seem to evade an investigation of matters laid against him.

The final action of a church, as to an accused minister, may take any one of the following forms:

1. That of an *acquittal*, where no fault worthy of further consideration was proven against him; the charges were not sustained, and he is pronounced innocent.

2. That of *admonition:* To caution and admonish him to greater circumspection may be all which the case requires.

3. That of a *withdrawal of fellowship from him as a minister of the gospel*, with a declaration that in their opinion he is unworthy of, and unfit to continue in, the ministerial office. This may be done, and the man still be retained in the fellowship of the church as a private member. There may be faults

which would disqualify him for the exercise of a public ministry, but might not unfit \` 1 for private membership. Such an act of disfe. .wship as a minister would virtually be an act of deposition from the sacred office, so far as any act of church or council could depose him.

4. That of the *withdrawal of fellowship from him as a church member*, thus excluding him from the body. This, accompanied with a declaration of his unworthiness as a minister of the gospel, constitutes the final and utmost act of the church's disciplinary power, in such a case. They can do no more. This puts him out, and deposes him from the ministry, so far as any human power can depose him. It also clears the church from any further responsibility as to his character or conduct. His disfellowship as a *member* adds emphasis to his disfellowship as a *minister*.

To the above-named acts a council may advise; but the acts themselves, to be valid and of any force, must be the acts of the church and not of the council. It would be an impertinent assumption for a council to attempt such an exercise of ecclesiastical authority.

By-Laws
Mt. Calvary Missionary Baptist Church
Page Two

The pastor shall serve as moderator of the church and shall preside at all business meetings of the church and at all meetings of the Advisory Council.

Termination of the Pastorate: The term of office maybe ended upon ninety(90) days notice on the part of the pastor or of the church. Termination of the office shall be voted on at a special called meeting. Notice of such meeting and its purpose are to be read from the pulpit on two successive Sundays. The presence of at least three deacons and the majority of the members present and qualified to vote shall make valid the termination of said office.

III. BOARDS AND COMMITTEES

Evangelism Committee: It This committee shall seek to win souls to Christ. It should plan special evangelistic visitation and meetings through which the church reaches out to those out side of the church.

Music Committee: The musical program of the church is entrusted to this committee. It is made up of the choristers of each choir, organists, minister of music, choir directors, and other music staff members.

Auditing Committee: The committee is responsible for reviewing the financial records of the church at least once a year and to report its findings to the church at its Annual Meeting following the Treasurer's Report. It should be composed of persons other than the treasurer, financial secretary, and the board of trustees.

Pulpit Committee: When the pastoral office becomes vacant for any reason, this committee will be elected by the congregation. Instructions for the guidance of the pulpit committee should be sought from the State Convention Headquarters.

Advisory Council: It includes all of the officers of the church, the chairpersons of boards and committees and the presidents of auxiliary organizations. It sees that the many interests and responsibilities of a church are adequately provided for in the church program, and it works the varied objectives in to a coherent plan.

The Board of Deacons: The board should be made up of men of honest report, full of the Holy Spirit and wisdom. They should be present in Sunday School and at the mid-week Prayer and Bible Study service. They should be chosen by a free vote of the church and are to be faithful, prudent, experienced, and devout men. They are to have charge of the sick and needed members and also to act as counselors and assistants to the Pastor in protecting, overseeing, and advancing the general interest of the church.

There was no response to the lawyer's correspondence. They completely ignored it, but Thursday morning around ten o'clock, the chairman called and said, "Reverend, we want to know if we can come over this afternoon to talk to you and your wife?"

I said, "Yes, I'll be here, but I can't guarantee you that my wife will be here." Why didn't you call last night or earlier this morning before she went to work?"

I knew he was just creating a cover story to tell the church that they tried to talk to us but we wouldn't cooperate. I went on to tell him that I did not know what time my wife would be home, but he could call her at her job and ask her if she would be willing to meet with them.

I then asked, "Why aren't you abiding by the church bylaws?"

He answered me with this incredible statement, "The church ain't got nothing against you."

Again I asked, "Why aren't you abiding by the church bylaws?"

Then he said this, which was even more incredible, "Oh, you're trying to get me," and abruptly hung the phone up.

Meanwhile, I believe it was about ten o'clock that night when a member called. I knew right away she had bad news because of the tone of her voice. She said that they did meet tonight. The moderator was there and several board members from the association.

It was chaotic, she said. Some of the members wanted to know what were they voting on. Others wanted to know why weren't the bylaws being followed, and some asked, where is the pastor?

According to her, that went on for a long time, and finally one of the deacons yelled out, "Let's vote! Let's vote!" At which time the moderator ended the discussion. Then she said, some of the deacons started passing out the ballots, some people did not take one.

When they finished voting they took them in the back and came back and announced the result. She said they said the result was sixty-one to dismiss and fifty not to. Before the meeting was adjourned she said the chairman spoke to the members and chastised them for their unruly behavior, and somebody yelled out in disgust regarding the wrongness of it all, and she said, he begrudgingly said, "Well, you all don't know what his wife told us."

The next day I received this certified letter from the church, and a check for what was supposed to have been my ninety-day severance pay. Of course it was the incorrect amount, and I took it along with the letter to my attorney.

Mount Calvary Missionary Baptist Church
924 North Eighth Street
Wilmington, North Carolina 28401

January 18, 2002

Reverend C. H. Reddrick
1801 Brierwood Road
Wilmington, North Carolina 28405

Dear Reverend Reddrick,

This letter is to inform you that the Board of Deacons of Mount Calvary Missionary Baptist church, called a special meeting on Thursday evening, January 17, 2002, with the congregation to make a decision if you should remain pastor of this church of if you should be dismissed.

Dr. Andre' Carr, Moderator of the Middle District Association presided over the meeting, along with Dr. Herring and deacon Alex Cox.

The voting was done by secret ballot.

The decision was for you to be dismissed from the Mount Calvary Missionary Baptist Church as pastor.

Please contact deacon George Vereen, chairman of the board at your earliest convenience to pick up your personal belongings from the pastor's study. Otherwise, you should not be on church property.

If you need further information please contact the chairman of the deacon board.

Respectfully,

George Vereen
George Vereen, Chairman of Deacon Board

Kenneth Drakford
Kenneth Drakford, Secretary of Deacon Board

Rena Lennon
Rena Lennon, Church Clerk

Publicly disgraced, humiliated and now unemployed, while still under intense internal and external attack, I felt the sorrow of defeat. It is hard to mount an offense against an enemy when you're under attack inside and out at the same time. I felt immobilized. How was I going to pay attorney fees? How was I going to pay my own bills? In addition to all of my other anxieties, I now had new ones piled on top of them. My load was heavy. My weeping was tarrying for nights and days. Often my wife was an eyewitness to my grief.

She would comfort me like a loving mother comforts her beloved child in moments of severe pain. When my weeping subsided she would say, "No I didn't catch you in bed; they lied on me when they said that, but you know you did it, and your own grandchild saw it. You brought all of this on yourself. You tore up the family."

Our home, which had witnessed many years of joyous events, had now become my private torture chamber. Yet, while often visited by hopelessness, it was the vision of the pick ax that wouldn't let it stay too long. It was in one of those moments of inspiration and determination that I decided to call an acquaintance of mine, who was a pastor of a local church and a member of the same association as my church. He was also on the executive board of the association. I admired him because he was different from most of the leaders in the association. He took the scripture seriously; he believed in enforcing the rules; and he was very spiritual.

He asked, "Reverend why did your wife go to the deacons?"

I answered, "I don't know; I believe she's sick. None of it is true."

"I just don't believe a church should be in court," he said.

He continued, "In a fair election you would win by a landside. Did the church vote to authorize the association to conduct that election?"

I told him that I did not know as I was not there at the close of the service.

"We can solve this problem without going to court," he added.

Then he said, "Reverend, I am going to call the moderator and find out."

In less than an hour he called me back and said, "Reverend, the moderator took the chairman's word for it. That meeting is illegal. You call the members, better yet, you have some of the members call as many members as they can and tell them that the moderator, and the board will be returning to the church to nullify that meeting on Thursday the 24th at 7pm."

This was Tuesday, the 22nd when we spoke. I was ecstatic. I told him to make sure that the association put their statement in writing. I carried out his instructions. The next day some of the members called and said that the deacons were telling members that there would not be a meeting at the church on Thursday night, but on Thursday evening the moderator and several board members came to the church along with a large number of the members and some of the deacons and trustees. Noticeably absent was the chairman. The doors were locked and new locks had been installed. The deacons and trustees who were there tried to persuade the moderator not to have the meeting, but to no avail. Under a street light near where the new sanctuary was being built, the meeting was called to order. After prayer, the moderator gave his purpose for being there, and then read the statement. Copies were passed out to all of those who were there. The meeting was then turned over to me. I thanked the moderator and the board, had prayer, gave the benediction, and we all left.

MIDDLE DISTRICT BAPTIST ASSOCAITON
407 N Wright St.
Burgaw, NC 28425

January 24, 2002

Mt. Calvary Baptist Church
924 N 8th St
Wilmington, NC 28401

Dear Pastor Reddrick & The Mt. Calvary Church Family:

    This letter is to certify that the meeting that was held on Thursday, January 17, 2002, with the members of Mt. Calvary Baptist Church was an unofficial meeting. The Moderator and the executive board feel as though we were misinformed. Therefore, all action items at this particular meeting are considered null and void. Dr Andre Carr, the Moderator of the Middle District Association, was contacted by Deacon Vereen and asked to come and preside over a meeting at Mt. Calvary. Dr. Carr asked the following questions:

1. Have you talked to your pastor?
2. Are the church members aware of this meeting?
3. Will the church clerk verify this request for a meeting?

The answer to question # I was, "we tried but he wouldn't talk with us." The answer to the next two questions was "yes." Therefore, based on the given information Dr. Carr and the members of the executive board acted in accordance. It was made clear by the Moderator that we will only act with regards to the voting issue. By no means did the executive board or the moderator intend to disregard the pastor. Since then the board has been informed that all members were not contacted, and told specifically that they would be voting on retaining or dismissing their pastor.

It is the policy of the association to act only when we have been called upon and that call is the consent of the church family and the pastor. We understand that the pastor was not even aware of this meeting.

Since the above-mentioned rules were broken, the association deems that this meeting was not in accordance to the by-laws of the association.

For the Cause of Christ,

Rev. Dr. Andre Carr, Sr. Moderator

Rev. Terry L. Henry, Acting Secretary

With the meeting now nullified, by the very ones who did the presiding and the conducting, it was indeed a major victory. And the strong denunciation of the chairman's conduct was an unexpected surprise. It was additional proof of his dishonesty and a clear demonstration of the extent that he was prepared to go to have me destroyed.

However, a statement made by one of the association board members to the group upon leaving, gave me some concern. He said, "The association is now out of this. This matter is now in the hands of Reverend Reddrick, and the members of Mt. Calvary Baptist Church."

We were now left to fight it out on our own, while they watched from the sidelines. But I was grateful for what they'd done, and my opinion of my friend had been validated. I was glad that I'd called.

The next day in consultation with my attorney, the decision was made to interview my wife. She agreed, and the interview took place the next day, Saturday morning, in his office. While I waited in the waiting room, the two of them went in the conference room next door. After what seemed like three hours, my wife finally emerged with a document for me to read. She asked me for my opinion. I told her I thought it was fine, with the exception of one minor error that I thought needed correcting. Before she left to go back in, I asked her why it was taking so long? She said she wanted to make sure that it said what she wanted it to say, and that the lawyer was a slow typist.

When that minor correction was made, we left there to get the document notarized. This was my wife's statement, and she wanted it to be read to the congregation on Sunday morning. In his final remarks to me before we departed the attorney said, "Reverend, when you go to that church tomorrow, you preach the best sermon you've ever preached."

STATE OF NORTH CAROLINA

<u>**AFFIDAVIT**</u>

COUNTY OF NEW HANOVER

The undersigned, first being duly sworn deposes and says as follows:

1.   I am the wife of Rev. Chester H. Reddrick, pastor of Mount Calvary Missionary Baptist Church. The purpose of this affidavit is to set forth the true facts about what I supposedly said regarding my husband Chester Reddrick.

2.   My husband and I had a personal problem, and I felt I had to talk to someone. My husband suggested talking to one of the church deacons. I decided to talk with Mr. George Vereen, the Chairman of the Board of Deacons at our church. Deacon Vereen promised that the conversation between us would be totally confidential.

3.   I understand from my husband that Deacon Vereen called a Deacon's meeting without my husband, the Pastor, present and told the Deacons that I had told him I had caught my husband in bed with another woman. My husband said he learned this from Deacon Vereen in a later Deacons meeting when Deacon Vereen again violated the confidential nature of our discussion and misstated what I said before the Deacons and before my husband. I want to emphasize that I never said any such thing, and that the problems my husband and I had were private in nature and I expected any conversations I had with anyone about my problems to remain private.

4.   I met my husband when I was 18 years old. My husband and I have been married for over 30 years and he has served in the ministry for over 25 years. We have two children. He is an honorable and Christian man, and I believe he has been good for our church I believe that it was wrong that he was discharged this past Thursday, January 17, 2002, especially without an

opportunity to properly defend himself before the congregation and against the accusations which have been made against him.

5.   I am signing this affidavit with the understanding that, though it may be read to others, no copies of it will be made or distributed, other than the original and one other copy made at the time of signing.

Further affiant saith not.

Loraine Reddrick
LØRAINE REDDRICK

Sworn to before me on

this the 26 day of January, 2002

Maria C. Hall
NOTARY PUBLIC

My Commission Expire 6·28·06

MARIA C. HALL
NOTARY
—
PUBLIC
NEW HANOVER COUNTY, N.C.

On Sunday morning, I did not get the chance to preach the best sermon I ever preached nor did I get the chance to have my wife's affidavit read. It was my wife's opinion that it would be better if someone else read the affidavit rather than her. She felt that she would not be able to maintain her composure under the circumstances; therefore, the decision had been made to have either the church clerk read it or someone else.

At any rate, when I arrived at the church, I noticed that there were deacons and trustees standing in the doorway at the side entrance where I usually entered the sanctuary. When I got out of the car and walked toward the door to enter, the chairman came down the steps and met me before I got to the steps.

"You are not allowed to come in here," he said.

"The association has nullified that meeting," I answered.

"We don't care. The association has no authority over us," was his response.

Then from the group somebody said, "Call the police!"

I waited there for the police to arrive. Meanwhile, I began talking to some of the members who were arriving for Sunday morning worship. Two men, staunch supporters of mine noticed the altercation and came over and stood with me, while I waited. One of them was growing increasingly more furious, but I remained calm and urged him to do likewise. I told him that we did not want to create a disturbance, but that we would wait until the police arrived.

I had no intention of fighting my way into the sanctuary, and it was clear that if I were going to get in there that morning that would be my only way in. Of course I was not about to leave as if I was a criminal who'd broken some law, nor was I about to give them the slightest impression that I was afraid. I knew that this was a spiritual war that I was engaged in, and the enemy that was standing before me was the enemy of God. When the police eventually arrived, I walked over to his car joined by one of the members who waited with me, I told him who I was, thanked him for coming, and told him that his services were not needed. He left. Then I got in my car and also left.

A few days later, my attorney went before a judge and got a temporary restraining order to allow me back in the pulpit until the preliminary hearing on the lawsuit was held. The church attorney filed a counter suit against that. A hastily arranged hearing was then arranged by the two lawyers, and the judge to decide the matter. I did not fully understand the legal arguments that were hurled back and forth in front of the judge.

When the judge summoned both lawyers to his bench for a quick conference, I heard him say this to my attorney, and in a not too friendly tone, "You didn't tell me this earlier." I felt that it had something to do with the slander, because from that point onward, the judge agreed with every argument put forth by the church's attorney. He discreetly and effectively wrapped the deacon's allegations around his arguments and made it appear that my return back in that pulpit would be a danger to the church. The judge nodded in agreement with his every word. When my attorney responded, it was clear that he had no weapons in the arsenal of his arguments to turn the tide. The temporary restraining order was revoked. My hopes went down in defeat. In spite of having the association's ruling and my wife's affidavit, it appeared that none of it mattered. I had no confidence now that the outcome at the preliminary hearing would be any different. The judge didn't appear to be favorable at all, the church attorney was bold and confident, and my own attorney acknowledged to me that we would have a tough hurdle to overcome on the issue of irreparable harm.

Of course, my premonitions were correct; the preliminary hearing was a rerun of the hearing on the temporary restraining order. It was like walking in a lion's den. The church attorney even asked one of the witnesses, "What was the rumor around the church concerning the pastor?"

Thank God, she was noble enough of character not to answer it. The chairman testified, that the church did not have bylaws. The ruling of the judge was that I would not suffer irreparable harm by staying out of the pulpit until the lawsuit was settled.

Away from the courtroom and now back at my attorney's office, I told him that I wanted to drop the lawsuit. I didn't think that I could win. Furthermore, I told him that I was now unemployed and with no immediate prospect for employment. Plus I said, "I already owe you a sizable amount of money that I don't even know how I am going to pay." He pleaded with me not to drop the suit.

He said, "Reverend, if you do that it'll be like General Lee moving his cannons from in front of Grant's army." I thought his metaphor strange, but I got his point. He urged me to let him work towards a settlement. He was confident that his firm would allow him to work on it in his spare time, thus reducing my cost.

He was compassionate and kind, and I told him that I would think about it and let him know when I decided. Then he reminded me of something that I was well aware of, "You know it was your wife that started all of this."

After leaving the attorney's office, I started thinking about the scene in the courtroom. The church was definitely divided between those who supported the pastor, those who supported the deacons, and those who just stood on the sideline not knowing who to support. I thought how sad a scene that was. Some of those people who stood with the deacons now were some of our best friends just a few weeks ago. Even the deacons were considered our best friends.

But there was something else that I noticed that day in the courtroom that was even more amazing than all of the other shifts. There was a former member there who'd had the right hand of fellowship removed from him about five years ago. He'd repeatedly violated the church covenant and bylaws and refused to be reconciled. He hated the deacons and me. In the courtroom that day I noticed that he and the deacons had reconciled, had set aside their differences and had joined forces against their common foe.

meeting was conducted by a nonmember moderator mutually chosen by the parties. At the meeting, 112 members were qualified to vote, voting 40 in favor of readmission, and 72 against.

8. Plaintiff church has a specified process in which members can become reunited with the church and readmitted as a member. The reconciliation process is a voluntary process, requiring that the excluded member confess his or her fault, accept the chastisement of the church leaders, and be readmitted upon a majority vote of the church.

9. None of the Defendants have attempted to reconcile with the church by going through the steps of reconciliation.

10. Neither the pastor of the church nor the church conducted themselves in an extreme or outrageous fashion toward the Defendants, nor have the Defendants suffered any emotional distress. The Defendants presented no evidence of any damages as a result of any alleged emotional distress.

Based on the forgoing FINDINGS OF FACT, the Court makes the following:

CONCLUSIONS OF LAW

1. The Court has jurisdiction over the parties and the subject matter herein, and the parties are properly before the Court.

2. The issue of the Defendants' termination of membership, having been determined by a majority of the voting membership of the church, the Defendants should be bound by the decision of the church. The Court should not inquire into matters of a purely ecclesiastical nature, but the Court may properly review the process followed by the church as it relates to the Church Covenant, By-Laws and the Hiscox Manual.

CHAPTER 3

Refuge In A Mosque

With the preliminary hearing now over, the stigma of the slander still attached to me like a corpse: with no peace in the home, with no income coming into my accounts, now depleted due to my growing expenses, it was more than obvious to me that my troubles would not be ending soon. I was in a protracted war, and God knows how long it would last. It was the vision and some loyal supporters that still sustained my hope. One day one of them called and wanted to know if it was alright with me if they met for prayer. I told her, "Of course, yes." Although, I was beginning to feel that I didn't want to have anything else to do with the church, I agreed to go because of their continued faith in me. At the meeting that night, a ninety year old saintly mother said to me, with tears rolling down her cheeks, "Reverend, I'm going to guarantee you myself that you won't go hungry." While she was saying that she put forty dollars in my hand and said with certainty, "Take this Reverend; some more will be coming next week." Her grandson's wife followed her and stuffed some money in my hand as well. Others arbitrarily did the same thing that night. Before the meeting was closed, a decision was made by the group to have weekly prayer meetings at a location to be announced at each weekly meeting. My wife attended that first meeting and seemed to be supportive of the group's intentions. Her income now was the only certain income coming into the home and for a brief period that reality was the basis of our unity.

In the meantime, as I continued to mobilize my efforts to economically survive, a thought occurred to me that I might be able to borrow a loan against one of my retirement accounts. I called and discovered that I could. At the next weekly prayer meeting the supporters who came paid their tithes and offerings and some who didn't, sent some money. A treasurer was elected and that night I went home with far more money than I did the first week.

I am sure that there was a church somewhere in the city or surrounding area that would have welcomed me had I come for worship. Several preachers called and said that they were in prayer for us. But my wounds were open wounds and I felt that I could not endure the additional pain of judgmental stares that I knew I would receive from some people. One such incident took place at a store that I entered. A minister's wife that I knew was leaving as I entered. When she looked at me, she frowned, and dropped her head disapprovingly. Trying to mask my shame and pain, I spoke to her, "The truth of this matter will be coming out soon." She paused and without saying a word went on about her business. I tried to protect myself from the pain of such public rebukes by not going to places that I was accustomed to going. I stopped speaking to people unless they spoke to me first. I did my best to insulate myself from the ridicule and shame by going into a self imposed exile in my own community.

That was one of the reasons I was motivated to call a mosque late one Sunday evening. Additionally, I'd been frustrated for a long time with Christians who seem to have no intentions of living their lives governed by their professed beliefs. What was happening to me was proof of that. I thought to myself, "How could these church people, treat my family and me with such cruelty? How could they so easily swallow gossip and rumors? How could they deny another human being basic human rights?"

When the man at the mosque answered the phone, I asked him if there would be service that evening. He said there would be evening prayer. He told me the time and I went. When I got there the same gentlemen warmly greeted me. That's when I discovered that he was African American. On the phone he had an accent so his nationality was not obvious to me. He introduced himself to me, directed me to a place on the floor and then gave me a pamphlet to read. I had already removed my shoes.

Only that gentleman was there, the Imam, and another man. They all greeted me and continued in their reading. I had arrived before the designated time of prayer. The atmosphere was quiet, sacred and peaceful. For a long time I'd been curious about Islam and its faith. For some strange reason I felt comfortable there. As I sat in the floor reading, I was relieved to know that nobody there knew me. Nobody looked at me disapprovingly. Nobody asked me who I was and why I was there. This seemed like a perfect place of refuge.

When some of the other men arrived, they each warmly greeted one another—including me—in their traditional Islamic way. And when the time came for their evening prayer, the Imam led the ritual. I remained seated on the floor in deference and quiet meditation. The ritual prayer was sacred and moving, although I didn't have a clue as to what was being said. It was all in Arabic. Most of the men were of Middle Eastern origin with the exception of a few who were African American.

After the evening prayer was over, the gentleman that I talked to on the phone and who had greeted me when I arrived told me when they met again. I thanked him and told him that I would be back. I left feeling comforted by their warmth and kindness and looked forward to returning. This would be my spiritual shelter in my storm, my hiding place and my place of refuge.

The Bible says, "The earth is the Lord's the fullness thereof the world and those that dwell therein." It didn't matter to me that this was a mosque. I found love there. Down the street from our home was a little Assembly of God Church. I went there on several occasions to their night service. The pastor and his wife were Canadians. I told them my sad story. They prayed for me and I was also comforted by their genuine concern.

About the middle of February my oldest brother, along with his wife and daughter, came to the house for a visit. They lived out of town and often came to visit a dear aunt, some cousins and of course us. When he came in the house that day the first thing he said is what he always says when he greets me, "How are things going fella?"

I responded in great sorrow, "Haven't you heard?"

He said, "No, heard what?"

I had assumed that our aunt or our cousin had told him already. But I discovered that they hadn't; therefore, I started from the beginning telling them what had happened. In the middle of the story my brother interrupted me and said, "The more you describe this the more it sounds like Andrae Yates."

He continued, as if in a trance, "Your wife is sick. It's a wonder you haven't committed suicide. A lot of people faced with what you've gone through would have committed suicide."

Then he went on to tell me why he was so certain of her illness. He told me that for years he'd been a member of the board of directors of the Mental Health Department in the city where they lived and that he'd seen that kind of illness quite often. His description of my wife's behavior was so vivid and exact that I could have sworn that he had access to a hidden camera somewhere in the house.

He went on to say this to me, "You're in the Bible. Read Job. God must have something for you to do. You go ahead and do what God told you to do."

And then, he said, "Be kind to your wife, she's sick and can't help it."

For the first time now, since all of this started, I was finally in the presence of someone who understood and diagnosed my wife's condition. Because my brother is older than me, our worldview was often different on various subjects. Down through the years, in our many debates, I often felt that he thought that I should submit to his views primarily because he was the elder. But that day in our home all of that dissipated, like a vapor in the air. Here was my oldest brother, stooping down to tenderly minister to me. He bathed my wounds in the healing waters of his wisdom and unconditional love. I would never see him in the same light again. That day he was a ministering angel sent from God.

A few days later, my wife and I agreed that we needed professional help. She recommended going back to the counselor that we both visited earlier but I insisted that we see a psychiatrist. I told her that my brother had visited while she was out but did not tell her the nature of the conversation. She agreed with me and told me to make the appointment. The next day I got busy trying to get an appointment. I used the yellow pages; everywhere I called they were all booked for days and weeks in advance; however, one secretary was nice enough to have her boss, who was busy when I called, to call me back. When he called he told me that it would be weeks before he would be available to see us, but he gave me the phone number of a psychiatrist who had recently opened an office in the city. He suggested that I try there. I did and got an afternoon appointment for the next day.

My wife met me there. When we entered his office, he greeted us and wanted to know how he could help us. I told him that my wife believed that I had an affair with our grandson's mother and that I'd lost my job because of her false allegations. Then I told him that we needed his help to unveil the truth.

He then asked me to leave the room so that he could talk to my wife alone. I went back to the waiting room.

After what appeared to have been forty to forty five minutes, my wife came out and said, "He wants to see you now." I went in and he asked for the names of two people that knew both of us very well. I gave him the names of two ladies from the church. He then asked me to have my wife return. When she did, he told her that he'd asked me for the names of two people that knew both of us very well. He told her the names that I'd given him and asked her did she have any objections to them. She said she did and he then asked her for two people. She paused and said, "I can't think of anyone." But then she agreed that it was alright for the psychiatrist to speak to one of the persons I suggested. He then told us that he would have us to return a few days later to take a series of tests. He explained the nature of the test to us; we made the appointment and left.

When we got back home from the appointment, my wife was agitated and started complaining about the place and the doctor. I tried to allay her anxieties; however, when she left for school the next morning her departing words to me were, "Call that man and tell him that if he talks to that woman, I will not be coming back for that appointment."

Later that day when I finally got the chance to speak to the doctor, I told him what my wife said. He said to me, "Reverend, I knew your wife was not coming back. Your wife is a sick woman and needs treatment. She's psychotic delusional, but you come on to the appointment Friday even if she doesn't come."

Then he said, "Those tests that I'd planned to give on Friday would have proven it, but I've had enough experience to recognize it when I see it."

Then he continued by saying, "That's a shame what those people at that church did to you." He even told me that he would be willing to meet with the church to explain his opinion.

After talking with the doctor, I felt both joy and sorrow. Sorrow that my wife was sick but joy that a professional had now confirmed what my brother had already said. I told my supporters what I thought was good and bad news. They cried with me and rejoiced with me at what we all thought was the kind of news that would unravel the whole saga.

In the meantime, on the night of our next prayer meeting the weather turned awful and the meeting was canceled. That caused me considerable anxiety because I'd come to depend on the weekly tithes and offerings to survive economically. But the next day, when I went to the mailbox, there was a letter there from a noble preacher. This man is a true believer and a dedicated and consecrated soul. He'd been calling me daily now encouraging me in the Word, not to give up, not to leave the church and not to join the Muslims. His convictions were the same as another beloved minister who was also ministering to me at the time. They both thought that for me to become a Muslim was the worse thing that I could do. When I opened the letter a five hundred dollar check was enclosed. I was in awe, and asked myself, *What motivated this majestic soul to give me such a needed gift?*

It was that gift that day that ignited a new fire of determination in my soul not to give up and to keep fighting to clear my name. I got that check on Friday, and two days later, as a matter of fact, on Sunday night a very strong impulse came over me to get a private investigator. I opened the phone book looked in the yellow pages and the first name I saw under private investigator, I called. It was Sunday night, and reason said, *Ain't nobody there.*

But the Spirit said, "Call!"

When a man answered, I was surprised. I told him my dilemma, and he said, that he didn't take cases involving churches, but I persisted and then he told me to meet him at his office the following morning. When I got there, I told him the full story and gave him some of the documents I had. He said to me, "Reverend, if I did not believe you I would not take this case."

He told me his fee. I gave him a portion of that gift the minister had given me as a down payment. When I left, he said, "Reverend, the first place I'm going is to that deacon that your wife talked to." The following report is the private investigator's full report.

	DATE OF CONTRACT: February 28, 2002	FILE NUMBER 022802	
CLIENT	Chester Reddrick	SUBJECT	Mount Calvary
	1801 Briarwood Road		Missionary Baptist
	Wilmington, NC		Church
	910-799-3024		924 N. 8th St., Wil., NC

TYPE OF INVESTIGATION:

Slander/Defamation/Wrongful Termination

PREDICATION

On Thursday, February 28, 2002, this agency met with, pastor of the Mount Calvary Baptist Church in Wilmington, North Carolina. The Reverend Reddrick stated he had been dismissed as pastor of the Mount Calvary Baptist Church without cause. Reddrick stated that on Sunday, January 13, 2002, he arrived at Mount Calvary Baptist Church at his normal time. He was greeted by several members of the Board of Deacons and Board of Trustees. Deacon George Vereen was the main spokesperson.

The Deacons and Trustees informed the Reverend Reddrick that he would not be allowed to preach from the pulpit on this particular Sunday. They informed him he was being suspended as pastor until an accusation against him could be resolved. Reverend Reddrick was not allowed to preach that Sunday.

On Thursday, January 17, 2002, the Board of Decons and Trustees met with part of the congregation of the church to determine Reverend Reddrick's future. The church meeting was moderated by the Dr. Andre Carr, Sr., and a reverend of the Middle District Baptist Association, 407 North Wright Street, Burgaw, North Carolina 28425. The church was asked to vote upon the continuation of as pastor of the church. With a vote of 60 voting to dismiss the pastor and 52 voting to keep the pastor, Reverend Reddrick was discharged from his duties.

Reverend Reddrick contends the church violated the Hiscox Guide for Baptist Churches by holding this January 17, 2002 meeting. The bylaws require that such actions against a pastor be made public with two preceding consecutive Sunday announcements from the pulpit. This was not done.

On Friday, January 24, 2002, Reverend Reddrick and the Mount Calvary Baptist Church received a letter from Dr. Carr, the moderator on the January 17, 2002 meeting. The letter condemned the January 17, 2002 meeting because "the moderator and the executive board feel as though we were misinformed." The letter further stated, "All action items at this particular meeting are considered null and void."

In addition to the absence of following the bylaws set forth by the Hiscox Guide for Baptist Churches, Reverend Reddrick says the allegations against him are a prefabricated lie. The Board of Deacons and Trustees has accused Reverend Reddrick of being caught in bed with a young female in his residence by his wife, Loraine Reddrick. She provided an affidavit stating that she never told the Board of Deacons, the Board of Trustees, or anyone else that she caught her husband in bed with another woman in their residence.

It is the mission of this investigating agency to interview and determine the facts concerning conversations between Deacon George Vereen and Loraine Reddrick. Additionally, this agency will employ investigative methods to determine if any member of the congregation was predisposed to their vote prior to January 17, 2002 to vote against the reverend. Additionally, many parishioners were uninformed as to the nature of their vote or the nature of the allegations when they were summoned to the church on January 17, 2002.

CHRONOLOGY OF EVENTS

On Friday, March 1, 2001 at 7:00 p.m. this Agency conducted a face to face interview with George Vereen at his residence at 1523A Cameron Court, Wilmington, NC. Mr. Vereen is the Chairman of the Deacons at Mount Calvary Baptist Church. He has been a member since the 1950s. Mr. Vereen was very agitated at being interviewed. He said Mrs. Reddrick came to him in confidence sometime in December before Christmas. He was asked exactly what did Mrs. Reddrick tell him. He became very agitated and responded, "I don't betray confidence." He was very agitated with the question and refused to answer. His only response was, "All this has been settled in court. Reddrick is out!" He was asked, if he did not betray her confidence, then how did the other Deacons know what to fire for. Vereen became agitated and referred all questions to the church attorney, Mr. Kenneth Stephens. Vereen loudly stated, "I'm sick of." As this Agency was leaving, Vereen was asked, "You don't like Reverend Reddrick very much, do you?" He responded very sharply, "He's done nothing to me personally."

On Monday, March 4, 2001 at 9:10 a.m. this Agency conducted a face to face interview with Ms. Rosetta Geddie at her place of employment, the Wilmington Housing Authority. Ms. Geddie has been on the Board of Trustees at the Mount Calvary Baptist Church since 1998. She has no personal knowledge of the exact words spoken to Deacon George Vereen by Mrs. Reddrick. She did not attend church on January 13 when the Deacons and Trustees met concerning Reverend Reddrick's suspension. No one called her to advise her this meeting of the Deacons and Trustees was to take place. She was shown the memo concerning this meeting of the Deacons and Trustees. She said she was aware of the memo, but still did not attend. She only know of hearsay. She had heard that Mrs. Reddrick had mentioned to William Nixon, a church Deacon, that she had a problem. Nixon told her to take it to Vereen since he is the Chairman of the Deacons. She said she did not even know the Thursday, January 17th meeting to vote on Reverend Reddrick's future except by word of mouth by supporters of Reverend Reddrick. Ms. Geddi said she did not know the allegations against Reverend Reddrick until the church meeting. Deacon Joseph Canty was the main person speaking. Ms. Geddie said he did not even inform the group exactly what Reverend Reddrick was accused of; nor did he offer any proof to the allegations. During the meeting, Willie Lee Brown stood up and told the church that the Deacons were trying to fire Reverend Reddrick because there was a rumor that he had an affair with a young lady in his home and Mrs. Reddrick had caught them in bed. To her knowledge, no member or a representative of the church ever did an investigation into the allegations against Reverend Reddrick. She recorded the vote at the church as 60 in favor of dismissal and 52 to retain Reverend Reddrick. She does not think there was an effort to get all the curch members together; but rather those who would vote to dismiss Reverend Reddrick. She recalls hearing part of a conversation while passing Deacon Vereen and Deacon Canty one Sunday. She was sure they were discussing Reverend Reddrick. Canty had a file folder in his hand. She heard Canty say to Vereen, "We know something is going on, but not what." Geddie says she has heard through hearsay that Canty did not care much for Reverend Reddrick. Ms. Geddie is a supporter of Reverend Reddrick and voted for him to remain as pastor of the church. She has never seen the Reverend display any type of behavior that would cause a reasonable and prudent person to conclude he is capable of being unfaithful to his wife.

On Sunday, February 10, 2002, the Board of Trustees and the church Deacons met to discuss running an advertisement to replace Reverend Reddrick. Ms. Geddie opposed the running of the ad because the termination of Reverend Reddrick had not been adjudicated in court. She also voiced her opinion that Reverend Reddrick had been dismissed without any proof of the allegations against him. She said the Deacons berated her for her views and opinions. There was a motion made to run the ad. She did not stay for the vote. She left and later discovered she had been discharged from the Board of Trustees.

On Wednesday, March 6, 2002 at 6:00 p.m. this Agency conducted a face to face interview with Willie Lee Brown at his residence at 513 Anderson Street. Mr. Brown is a strong supporter of Reverend Reddrick. He has been a faithful member of the Mount Calvary Baptist Church for the past three years. He said he knew of the allegation against Reverend Reddrick and the church meeting set for January 17 because Deacon Joseph Canty had visited him on Wednesday, January 16, 2002 in his home. Canty's visit was for the purpose of soliciting support to vote Reverend Reddrick out of the church on the next evening. Canty had told him Mrs. Reddrick had told Deacon Vereen that she caught Reverend Reddrick and a young woman having sex in the Reddricks home. The young woman is the mother of the Reddrick's grandson. Mr. Brown asked him about proof of the allegations. Deacon Canty did not answer him. Brown told him it was wrong for the Deacons to try to convince church members to vote Reverend Reddrick out of the church without any proof of an allegation. He told Brown he didn't care, that "we don't want him there no more."

Mr. Brown said he was present in church on January 6, 2002, and there was no announcement of a meeting concerning Reverend Reddrick's future at the church. On January 13, 2002 he recalls a commotion between Reverend Reddrick and the Deacons concerning his suspension from the pulpit. Reverend Reddrick did not preach that day. At the time, Mr. Brown did not know why.

On Thursday, January 17, 2002 Mr. Brown attended the church meeting called by the Deacons. He said Deacon Joseph Canty was the main spokesman. The meeting called for a vote of Reverend Reddrick's future at the church. Several members asked

Canty what the allegation was. He only responded that it was "very serious". No explanation of the allegation was given. No proof of the allegation or indication that anyone had investigated the allegation. Mr. Brown said he felt like the Deacons had conspired against Reverend Reddrick and had solicited support from members prior to the meeting to vote against him. When Canty would not tell the members what the allegation was, Brown stood up to speak. He said he told the congregation that the Deacons were accusing Reverend Reddrick of having an affair with a young lady and he was caught in bed with her by Mrs. Reddrick. He said the Deacons were using this allegation to fire Reverend Reddrick because they didn't like him. He told the congregation that there was never any proof or an investigation into the allegation. He told them that what the church was doing was wrong.

On Saturday, March the 9th, 2002, at 8:00 p.m., this agency conducted a telephone interview with Isaiah Thomas. Mr. Thomas is a trustee for the Mount Calvary Baptist Church. Mr. Thomas says that he grew up in the Mount Calvary Baptist Church and attends regularly. Mr. Thomas stated that he arrived at church late on Sunday, January 13th, 2002. He was not aware of what was going on until he observed several of the members, Trustees, and Deacons meeting in the fellowship hall. He said there appeared to be quite a commotion. He was aware that the Reverend Chester Reddrick did not go into the pulpit to preach that Sunday. He said he did not ask because it did not involve him directly. He said it was announced January the 13th that there would be a meeting of the church on Thursday, January the 17th of 2002 to determine the Reverend's future. He said he asked George Vereen about the accusation of Reverend Reddrick having an affair. He said Vereen told him, "I have no facts. Where there' smoke, there's fire." To this date, Mr. Thomas says he has no facts to support the allegations of adultery against Reverend Reddrick were true. He knows of no person affiliated with the church or independent of the church that conducted an investigation to determine if the facts were true.

He said that it was brought in such a large forum that he could not imagine such an allegation without there being something to it. When asked if he felt bad about voting to terminate Reverend Reddrick's employment at the church without any facts to support such a serious allegation, Mr. Thomas responded, "That may be something that I have to pay for."

On Monday, March the 11th, 2002, at 8:30 p.m., this agency conducted a telephone interview with Kenneth Drake, a Deacon in the Mount Calvary Baptist Church. Mr. Drake appeared to be agitated with this interview. He stated he was not in the fellowship hall with a meeting of the Deacons or the Board of Trustees discussing the future of Reverend. He said he attended another meeting. When asked about the other meeting, Mr. Drake abruptly said, "I cannot discuss this. You'll need to call my attorney."

On Monday, March the 11th, 2002, at approximately 8:45 p.m., this agency conducted a telephone interview with Mr. John Green, trustee with the Mount Calvary Baptist Church, who also functions as chairman of the trustee board. This agency asked Mr. Green about his involvement in the January 13th, 2002 meeting between the Deacons and Board of Trustees concerning Reverend Reddrick's future at Mount Calvary Baptist Church. Mr. Green stated that he attended no such meeting. I read a memo to Mr. Green, dated January 13th, 2002, which paraphrases the Deacons and Trustees met with the chairman of the Deacons on January 13th at 11:00 a.m. The purpose of the meeting was to ask Reverend to sit down from the pulpit with pay until the accusations against him had been resolved. The memo further stated that a motion was made by Deacon Joseph Canty, Sr. and seconded by Deacon James Aiken. Mr. Green was informed that the memo bore his signature next to his name. When asked if he signed the document, he abruptly stated, "You'll have to talk to my attorney about this. I can't talk to you anymore."

On Wednesday, March the 13th, 2002, at 4:30 p.m., this agency met with Nakia Brown at her attorney's office. Her attorney is Ms. Erma Johnson, 2803 Market Street, Wilmington, North Carolina

28403. Her telephone number is (910) 762-0098. With the consent of Nakia Brown and her attorney, the interview was tape-recorded. Ms. Brown states that she is the mother of the Reverend Chester and Loraine Reddrick's grandson. She says she has never been contacted by anyone from the Mount Calvary Church who is a member of the Board of Deacons or the Board of Trustees. She says she has never been contacted by an independent source representing the Mount Calvary Baptist Church on behalf of the Board of Deacons or Board of Trustees. She says she has never been contacted by a representative of the Mount Calvary Baptist Church on behalf of the membership. She said she learned of the rumor that she'd had an affair in the residence of Reverend through her mother. Her mother had told her that Mrs. Loraine Reddrick had caught the two of them in bed together. She says she has always enjoyed a good relationship with the Redrdricks prior to the rumor of this adulterous relationship. Since the rumor began, she has experienced some uneasiness between her and Mrs. Reddrick. Ms. Brown was given a list of names for the Board of Deacons. She states that she does not know any of the members of the Board of Deacons with the exception of Mr. James Aiken. She stated that during high school she knew Mr. Aiken's son. When given a list of names of the Board of Trustees, she stated she did not know any of those people who were Trustees. She does not routinely attend the Mount Calvary Baptist Church. She says she has been hurt by the allegation because the rumor appears to have spread rapidly. She feels that some of her friends and co-workers look at her funny since this incident has arisen. She categorically denies that the allegations of an adulterous relationship between her and Reverend are true.

On Saturday, March the 16th, 2002, at approximately 8:20 a.m., this agency conducted a face-to-face interview with Mrs. Loraine Reddrick, wife of Reverend. Mrs. Reddrick said the day in question is December 7th, 2001. She said she observed something in her home that caused her to be suspicious of her husband's activities with Nakia Brown. This bothered her for several days. She said she went to George Vereen, chairman of the Deacons of Mount Calvary Baptist Church, in confidence. Vereen said he would take it to the

Deacons. Mrs. Reddrick objected and reminded him that what she said was in confidence. Vereen said, "Okay."

Mrs. Reddrick said she was at the school cafeteria of the Forest Hills Elementary School during her normal workday shortly before Christmas. William Nixon, a member of the Board of Deacons of Mount Calvary Baptist Church, was on the premises. His brother in-law is an employee of the school where Mrs. Reddrick teaches. Mrs. Reddrick was discussing her problem with several others at the cafeteria. William Nixon was part of the group to which she was talking. She says she denies ever telling anyone that she caught her husband in bed in their home with Nakia Brown. She said George Vereen and other Deacon members took what she had said, twisted it into their own words, and used the information to get rid of her husband as pastor of the Mount Calvary Baptist Church.

She said when she arrived at church on Sunday, January the 13th, 2002, the Deacons meeting in the fellowship hall appeared to be mad about something. She said they had this "evil look in their eyes." Since January the 13th, 2002, Mrs. Reddrick has received no phone calls, visits, or inquiries from any member of the Board of Deacons or Board of trustees concerning her well- being and welfare. She says it is as if "they got rid of my husband by using me and they don't need me anymore."

Mrs. Reddrick recalls, on an unspecified date, telling Anita Nixon, wife of William Nixon, that she did not appreciate her husband lying about Mrs. Reddrick saying she had caught her husband in bed with Nakia Brown. Anita Nixon denied that her husband ever made such a statement. Mrs. Reddrick assured this agency that she mentioned this concern of hers only to the chairman of the Board of Deacons, George Vereen, and Deacon William Nixon. She says she discussed it with no one else nor any member of the Board of Trustees. She says there has always been a small group in the church that resented the way the Reverend Reddrick ran the church. She says this was an opportunity for them to vote him out of employment. Then they could run things in the church like they want to.

On Friday, March 22nd, 2002, at 7:00 p.m., this agency conducted a telephone interview with Ms. Brenda Green, parishioner of the Mount Calvary Baptist Church. Ms. Green is the niece of Deacon Joseph Canty. Ms. Green grew up in the Mount Calvary Baptist church as a child. She moved away and returned in 1975 and has been very active in the activities and her attendance at the church since. She says she was in church on Sunday, January the 6th, 2002, and recalls there was no announcement of any type of meeting concerning the Reverend's future at the church.

On Sunday, January 13th, 2002, she says Reverend Reddrick did not preach in the pulpit. She said that the sermon was delivered by Patrice Canty. At no time, from the pulpit, was there any type of announcement that the church would need a meeting concerning Reverend Reddrick's future. She said there was a gathering or meeting after the church. Deacon George Vereen was the spokesperson. He said there were matters before the church that needed discussing and a date needed to be decided. Ms. Green said the conversation was very elusive and non-informative. She said she was so confused she left the meeting area and later came back. When she returned, she recalls Chester Sinclair, a parishioner, making a statement, "We need to do this quick." She said Deacon George Vereen and Deacon Joseph Canty agreed that the meeting would be Thursday night. She said there was no show of hands or any type of verbal vote to determine if Thursday, January the 17th, 2002, was amenable to everyone.

Ms. Green said she had heard through the "grapevine" that Reverend Reddrick had been caught in bed in his residence with Nakia Brown. She said she did not believe this. She says she has never seen anything in her 14 years of knowing Reverend Reddrick that would cause her or anyone else to think that he would engage in such conduct. She said while she was at church on January the 13th she asked Deacon Joseph Canty if anyone had talked to Nakia Brown to verify this incident. His response was, "Oh, my. We cannot do that." She asked why, and his response was, "We just can't." Ms. Green said this disgusted her, and she left.

On Thursday, January the 17th, 2002, Ms. Green attended the meeting at the church during her lunch hour. She thought the purpose of the meeting was to discuss the allegations against Reverend

Reddrick. She found out this was not true. She asked Deacon George Vereen what the meeting was about. Vereen's response was, "We're here to vote." She said he just walked on by her after that statement and barely spoke afterwards.

Ms. Green says she has had contact with Loraine Reddrick. She said on the afternoon of January the 13th after church she and Edith Miller went to the residence of Chester and Loraine Reddrick to visit. She said Mrs. Reddrick denied ever telling anyone that she had caught Reverend Reddrick and Nakia Brown in bed. She said Mrs. Reddrick appeared to be depressed. She said Mrs. Reddrick revisited the incident on December the 17th, 2001 and gave the following account. She said she came home and went into the garage. She observed Reverend Reddrick washing clothes. She went through a door from the garage into the den area. She observed Nakia Brown and her grandson watching TV. She told Ms. Green and Ms. Miller that the pastor "looked like he had just had sex." Ms. Green said she could tell that Mrs. Reddrick's demeanor was changing. She was very pleasant upon their arrival but became agitated as she told the story.

Ms. Green feels there is a clique in the church that operates more on a social level than a spiritual level. She says a lot of the parishioners did not like some of the changes that Reverend Reddrick had made in the church. She feels Deacon Joseph Canty is close to the people who resist the changes. She is positive that he and possibly others went to those people prior to January the 17th to solicit votes against Reverend Reddrick.

On Wednesday, March 27, 2002, at 1:50 p.m., this agency conducted a telephone interview with Ms. Francis Holliday. Mrs. Holliday is a long-standing member of the Mount Calvary Baptist Church. She stated that on January 17, 2002, she voted to dismiss Reverend Reddrick from his position at the church as pastor. She said she based this upon the conversation she had with Deacon George Vereen. Vereen had told her that Loraine Reddrick had visited Vereen in his home. The two of them drove off to be alone. While they were alone, Loraine Reddrick told Deacon Vereen that she had caught her husband in bed with Nakia Brown. Vereen had told Holliday that she should call Loraine Reddrick because she was "under the weather."

Ms. Holliday stated that she knew Loraine Reddrick and felt that she would never make up such a story. However, Holliday admits her vote was based solely on her conversation with Deacon Vereen. She recalls, on January 17, 2002, at the meeting, many people stated they did not now why they were there. She recalls Deacon Joseph Canty saying to a small group of people, "You know, fornication."

Ms. Holliday stated that she never heard anyone refer to an investigation into the matter to determine if it was true. To her knowledge, no investigation was ever done; but rather, the decision was based solely upon what Deacon Vereen was "telling people." Ms. Holliday said she always respected Reverend Reddrick and felt he was too intelligent for this.

She said she feels very sorry for Reverend Reddrick but is not sorry to see him go. She said the Reverend never showed much interest in senior citizens, such as her. She said he seemed to concentrate on the youth in the church.

Ms. Holliday is an elderly lady who lives in a Towers Apartment complex. She is dependent upon the church van to get her to and from the church. On January 17, 2002, Deacon Aiken drove the church van to her apartment complex to pick her up to carry her to the church. She said the meeting was passed around from mouth to mouth. She does not recall any announcement from the pulpit the previous two Sundays prior to January 17, 2002 concerning a meeting and the Reverend's future.

On Wednesday, March 27, 2002, at 5:45 p.m., this agency conducted a face-to-face interview with Benjamin and Oria McDaniel at their residence at 116 South 16th Street in Wilmington, North Carolina. Present at the meeting were the McDaniels' granddaughter, Shirley Nixon, and her husband, Anthony Nixon. The McDaniels are in their 90s. Oria McDaniel stated that on January 6th and January 13th that no announcement was made into the church concerning a meeting to determine the Reverend's future. She did attend the January 17th meeting. Benjamin and Oria McDaniels voted to keep Chester Reddrick as pastor of the Mount Calvary Baptist Church.

She said during the meeting no one announced the purpose of the meeting, and she did not know why she was voting.

Mrs. McDaniel says that it was some time after January 17th that Deacon Vereen and Deacon Aiken came by their house to visit. It was only then that they told the McDaniels that the reverend had been accused of having a sexual relationship with Nakia Brown. Mrs. McDaniels said that she did not believe that the reverend was capable of doing such a thing and could not understand why this could not have been discussed at the January 17, 2002 meeting. She asked Deacon Vereen "How do you know it's so?" Deacon Vereen's response was that Mrs. Reddrick had came to his house and told him.

Shirley Nixon stated that she was on the premises of Mount Calvary Baptist Church on Sunday, January 13, 2002. She recalls the Board of Deacons would not allow the reverend to preach that Sunday. She says no one knew why. She said after the church services there was a small gathering of some people at the church. Many were discussing a meeting slated for January 17, 2002. She did not attend the meeting nor did she remain on the premises to determine why. The McDaniels heard about the meeting through word of mouth. Deacon Aiken picked them up in the church van to transport them to the church for the January 17 meeting.

On Monday, April 8, 2002, at 8:45 p.m., this agency conducted a telephone interviews with Mattie Marshburn. Ms. Marshburn is extremely upset over the dismissal of Reverend Reddrick at Mount Calvary Baptist Church. She says she does not recall any announcement or discussion concerning a meeting on January 17, 2002. She knew of the meeting through Reverend Reddrick. There was no announcement on January 6th nor January 13th. She voted to keep Reverend Reddrick at the church as its pastor. She says the only thing she can see is that there is so much hatred by some at the church. She says that during the meeting no one told her why they were voting. She was never informed of the allegations against Reverend Reddrick. She says the Deacons and Board of Trustees did not act in the proper way to take actions against a pastor. She says he was treated like an animal after his dismissal. She recalls the Deacons attempting to grab Reverend Reddrick when he came to the church to retrieve some personal items. She said they had changed the locks on the doors of the church, causing some persons to have to meet outside. She says a lot of people have left the church over this unfortunate and evil act. Ms. Marshburn says she struggles to attend church at Mount Calvary Baptist Church because of this painful experience. At the January 17th meeting, she only recalls Deacon Canty and Deacon Vereen speaking to the parishioners before the moderator assembled the votes. She does not know exactly what Vereen and Canty were telling parishioners. She was never informed of the allegations against the reverend before she cast her vote.

SUMMARY

This investigation has shown that on about January 17, 2002 Reverend was dismissed from the Mount Calvary Baptist Church by a vote of approximately 60 for dismissal and 52 for retaining. This vote was moderated by a member of the Middle District Baptist Association. This investigation has shown that the Middle District Baptist Association has subsequently frowned upon the procedure used by the Mount Calvary Baptist Church to take actions against its pastor.

This agency has encountered several hostile witnesses who either refused to discuss the matter or referred the matter to an unnamed attorney. This agency has talked with numerous members of the congregation who claim they do not recall any of the bylaw formats being followed to dismiss the pastor of the church. Additionally, the same members do not recall ever being informed at the meeting of the allegations against its pastor. It is apparent through the investigation that some members of the congregation were solicited prior to January 17th to vote against keeping the pastor of the church. This agency has not talked with anyone for or against Reverend Reddrick who can describe the church going through the procedures of the Hiscox Guide for Baptist Churches for disciplinary action against a pastor.

It is the opinion of this agency that the following people would need to be deposed since they refuse to talk with this agency.

As I continued to visit the mosque on a regular basis, the gentleman who answered the phone initially became my friend. After one of their nightly prayers, the Imam spoke to the men for almost an hour about me. He was from Egypt and had not learned to speak much English at all. He spoke in Arabic and another man interpreted.

He said that I was of pure heart, a gifted speaker and that Allah had chosen me to be a Muslim. He said that when I took the suharta, my face would light up and the joy of Allah would fill my heart. He went on to explain the difference between choosing Allah and being chosen by Allah. Another brother there that night jokingly said to the Imam when he finished, "Dawn sheik, why you ain`t never said anything like that about me?"

I was amazed by the Imam's prophecy. I was also surprised that he'd characterized my personality so well. And in regards to my speaking, he'd never heard me speak publicly before, so how did he know I was a gifted speaker? I wondered. And my grief—*How did he know about tha*t, I thought. Did my face betray my attempts to hide my lingering grief?

At any rate the Imam was a reverent man and totally devoted to his faith. I was told that at the age of twelve he'd already memorized the Q'uran and would know if anyone misquoted one word of it. His final words to me that night were an open invitation for me to join the group in their ritual prayers and to attend the Friday service. I did both.

The sheik told me that when you bow down you're closer to God then, than at any other time. The other men treated me with the highest deference. One night one of them gave me a gift, his family Q'uran. It was written in both English and Arabic. I was very grateful.

After leaving the mosque one night after prayer, (there are five of them required each day and if they are prayed in the mosque there are special blessings to be received), my friend gave me a tape. I thought it was about Islam but when I listened to it, I discovered that it was a tape about Prepaid Legal. Immediately I decided to join. My thinking was that this would be a way to help me finance my legal battles.

I'd gotten the approval for the loan and would have the money soon. So I joined and requested an attorney. My friend was happy, and I was too but for totally different reasons. The appointment with the attorney was made, and I looked forward to the meeting. When I got the appointment letter, I noticed the attorney was not a local one. In fact he was located in another city, about sixty miles away. I felt a little uneasy about that. When I called to see if maybe they'd made a mistake, I was told that he was the closest one in my area proficient in handling my kind of case.

At the appointment, I gave him all of the documents that I had and an explanation of the events. I also told him that the case was being investigated and the investigator's name and phone number.

There was other conversation that take place with lawyer and client that of course took place between us. I gave him a retainer and left feeling that I would be well represented.

A few days later, at one of our weekly prayer meetings, someone asked this question, "Why wasn't the association doing something to enforce its ruling?"

It appeared to the group that the association had some moral obligation to vehemently defend the principle of the right that we were defending, more than just writing a letter nullifying the meeting.

"If the church was in violation of the association's rules, why was the church not held accountable for that violation by the association?" some asked.

In order to get some answers we all agreed to write the association for some answers and to express our sense of outrage over what appeared to us a lack of moral integrity on their part.

With my financial crisis now stabilized with a new attorney and with the diagnosis of my wife's illness—although not an official one—I now turned my attention to trying to get her into treatment. The psychiatrist was right; she did not return to her scheduled appointment. However, I went as he'd suggested. He reemphasized to me what he'd said to me on the phone earlier, which was that my wife was a sick women and in need of treatment as soon as possible. He also told me that if I needed help in coping with my tragedy that I could come there and someone on his staff would be there for me, free of charge. Again he expressed disbelief that church people could do such a thing as they had done to me.

He furthermore told me to have my attorney call him, and that he was available to testify or to help in whatever way he could to help me clear my name.

One of my strongest beliefs is the belief in family. That's one of my life's foundational principles. That's a part of who I am. I believe in a lifetime commitment to wife and children. I was raised that way. To me a family is like shock absorbers on cars, like great foundational pillars that hold up buildings, a nurturing place, a nesting place, a learning place, and a time out place. Therefore, there was no question in my mind about what I would do. I would do anything to get help for my wife.

Following the advice of friends and relatives, I called the local Mental Health Hospital and talked to a very sympathetic lady there. She was a nurse in charge of admittance in that department. I told her our problem and asked her for advice. She empathized with me and told me that they see that kind of condition quite often. She went on to tell me that there was medication available and that with proper diagnosis and treatment, most people, if they stayed on their medication can live quite normal lives. I told her that my wife refused to acknowledge her illness and therefore was not voluntarily seeking help. She then told me that an involuntary committal was the only way that I could get help for her. She told me what to do and it sounded so simple. I would discover that in my case at least, it was not that simple.

I discussed it with my attorney who was not certain of the legality of it. I discussed it with the psychiatrist; his position was that she needed treatment but not commitment. Neither one of them was totally confident of the outcome of this endeavor but was willing to support me if I proceeded. I, of course, was torn between doing something and nothing. I was also getting a lot of conflicting advice.

Some people would say, "This is your wife; you have an obligation to get help for her." That was true, but the other motivation moving me to act was the corpse on my back. I knew that if she returned to her right mind, I could take this thing off my back, bury it and be free again.

Therefore, I decided to go to the Clerk of Court's Office. When I got there I was handed a form to fill out. When I looked at the form I noticed that most of the questions did not apply to my wife's condition. I explained that to the secretary and told her the psychiatrist's opinion. She suggested that he send a notarized affidavit stating his basis for her committal. I felt then that my efforts were not going to bear fruit.

The psychiatrist had already told me that he did not think she needed to be committed, but that she needed treatment right away. He did, however, send an affidavit to the clerk of court. But the clerk ruled that her condition did not merit involuntary commitment. When my wife found out that I'd tried to get help for her, she misinterpreted my motives, and exploded into a rage like a volcanic eruption.

Her comment to me was, "You did this terrible thing, and now you're trying to cover it up by claiming that I'm insane. I can't stay with a wicked man like you. I am going to sue that psychiatrist and get a divorce."

The full fury of her wrath manifested itself a few days later when the doorbell rang. I went to answer it; it was a sheriff's deputy. He had a civil summons for me. When I read it, I felt like someone had just stuck a knife in my heart.

When I finished reading and evaluating the summons, particularly the grounds for divorce, I just couldn't believe what I was reading. I knew what the psychiatrist told me, and I knew that to be true, but still I couldn't understand how my wife could still be so effective in falsifying and manipulating events and people to my detriment. This added shame and the pain of being kicked out of the house would only compound my misery.

Later that evening when she got home from work, I approached her gingerly, like one would approach a bird in the wild. "Did you tell anyone that I was not contributing to the support of the home?" With eyes heavy with grief, she looked up at me as if startled by the question and said emphatically, "No, where did you get that from!"

I told her that I'd gotten the civil summons from her attorney and that it was one of her grounds for divorce. She then said that she did not tell that man that. I then left the room in a controlled but panic state of desperation. I went outside got the lawn mower and just started cutting the grass, all the while praying and wondering what I would do next.

In less than thirty minutes, out of my desperation came this idea; if I went to the hospital to have myself examined, maybe while there they would examine her too. I knew it was a ruse. But I was desperate. So I went back in the house and said to her, "I want you to take me to The Oaks." It didn't surprise me how willing she was to do so, because by now, my wife firmly believed that I was the one who was sick and needed help.

When I got to talk to the admittance nurse I told her my saga and told her that I was there to be examined to see if I needed help.

After asking me a few questions, she said, "Reverend you're fine, and I believe every word you're telling me."

At that very moment, I appealed to her to talk to my wife. She then told me in the most caring and sympathetic tone imaginable, that the only way they could help my wife, a doctor would have to admit her. I told her that in my wife's opinion nothing was wrong with her. She discussed with me some possible ways that I could get a doctor to authorize treatment for her; one of which I'd already tried. Then she said, maybe the doctor at the emergency room will do it. Try there.

Although, I knew it was a remote chance, I felt I had to try. In the waiting room she was fast asleep, partially covered by her coat to insulate herself from the chill of the room. When I woke her she asked me what had taken so long. I told her that the nurse did not think that anything was wrong with me. Then I told her that I had a terrible headache—which I did—and that I wanted the doctors at the emergency room to examine me. The latter was not the truth, but I was desperate and felt that I was justified in trying to get help for my wife.

The emergency room nurse cooperated with the hoax and after a lengthy waiting period, I got to see the doctor on duty that night. Again I told him my horror story. He listened with interest, and then said, he would be glad to help, but my wife refused to be examined. Because I so passionately appealed to him to do something, that man violated hospital policy and went out in the waiting room and talked to my wife there. When he returned to talk with me, he told me that he did talk to her and told her why I was there.

He then said that she told him that she was already seeing someone and that he had urged her to continue doing so. He told me that he was sorry, but that was all that he could do. I thanked him and left.

On the way back home now in the early hours of the morning, like flood waters, my wife's fury could not be contained. My acts of desperation only made matters worse.

At our weekly prayer meeting, I told the group about my new set of circumstances. They immediately called for fasting and prayer. With my new crisis also came a new legal challenge and liability. Two of my other brothers who had also been advising and encouraging me, thought that I should have a divorce attorney. The attorney handling my civil case handled divorce cases as well and was anticipating handling this one also. It would have been cheaper for me to have him do it. But they both were certain that it would be in my best interest to have another lawyer handle it. I finally agreed with them. Even though it meant more money coming out of my reserves, which was meant to last until this was over.

Meanwhile, I continued going to the mosque in the evening. But I also started going to the Friday prayer. There the Imam preached, and the mosque was full. I saw men there that I hadn't seen at the midweek prayer. As I sat there, I watched the fathers and their sons bowing down together, some toddlers, some preschoolers and some teenagers. The teenagers were just as concentrated in prayer as their fathers. What a marvelous sight. One little boy there, an African American, about the age of my grandson was there every Friday with his uncle. Sometimes he would bow when his uncle bowed; other times he would peep through his uncle's legs at me seated near the wall; at other times he would play with some other little boy his age, while his uncle and the other men continued in their ritual prayer. His little eyes were lit up with confidence. I took a special liking to him and always gave him little gifts with his uncle's permission. Through him, I vicariously fellowshipped with my grandson whom I was unable to see much now because of my wife's perverted belief.

I also met a white American man there. He was once a Catholic studying for the priesthood. But now he was a Muslim. There was also a young white college student there. I asked him one day how his family felt about him becoming a Muslim? He said they did not approve of it at all and mostly distanced themselves from him, with the exception of his grandmother whom he appeared to be close. His closest friend in the mosque was an African American young man whose goal was to study Islam in Saudi Arabia. His father was the man that answered the phone that first evening that I called the mosque. This strong male solidarity with its foundation in Allah, the Arabic name for God, was appealing to me.

Often on Friday as I sat watching this, I wondered if what happened to me in that church could happen to an Imam in a mosque. I also wondered that if my family had been raised Muslim would my sons have escaped the cultural rot that I tried so hard to isolate them from. Yes, I wondered if this religion with its emphasis on family values, morals, and its strict adherence to the teaching of the Q'uran was the road out of the graveyard of hopelessness and meaninglessness so prevalent among my people. And then the various cultures and nationalities gathered together in worship with no apparent inhibitions or barriers except language, was impressive to me.

And of course there were also occasions when we engaged one another in some controversial discussions. My friend considered himself my superior in the knowledge of Islam, because he was a Muslim and had been for years now, which I totally acknowledged. However, he did not know much about me at all or the extent of my education. He did not know, for example that I'd had some seminary training and was well read. There was no way he could have known. I remained an anonymous presence in their midst. I did that in order to escape the pain of my tribulation.

My friend also did not know that I was devouring the Q'uran like some fresh fruit never tasted before and for that reason probably knew more of its contents then he did. Although he was not a man with much formal education, he was kind to me and a very devout and dedicated Muslim. Because of all of these reasons I had great respect and admiration for him.

However, one night in an Arabic class that some of the men of the Mosque attended who didn't speak Arabic, a religious discussion took place that made me feel comfortable enough to tell the group about the vision of mine. Right after I told them, my friend spoke up in a moderate tone of condemnation and said, "Brother, that's the work of the devil; Allah don't send visions anymore," he said.

The teacher smiled and replied, "That's not correct, Allah sends visions to prophets, maybe he's a prophet." He was the same man that had given me the Beautiful Q'uran. My friend and the other men in the class that night accepted the teacher's correction without the slightest bit of resentment. He was their superior in the faith and they submitted to his wisdom without question.

I thought to myself, *Could I be a prophet?* Nevertheless, I began to talk a little more now but not much. I sensed that there were people in the Mosque, like people everywhere, some conservative and fundamentalist, and some opened minded and tolerant of different beliefs and traditions. But eventually some of the leaders became aware that I was a minister and would refer to me on some matters pertaining to the Bible. On one such occasion, one of them, who was a medical doctor, came to me and wanted my help in preparing a speech he had to give.

According to what he said to me it would be a speech to a non-Islamic audience. A speech centered around the account of Ishmael and his mother in the desert, when they were expelled from the home by Abraham. He told me that a white woman on the job told him that the well was in the Bible. He wanted to know from me was it true. I told him it was. He then asked me if I would show it to him. When I did, he was surprised. He was also surprised at the size of the Bible. He then asked me did I know the Bible like the Imam knows the Q'uran. I told him that I had not memorized it word for word but that I was knowledgeable of its contents. When I went on to tell him that the Bible was composed of many books, he was astounded.

A few weeks later at the Mosque one night, in a most caring spirit, he urged me to share with him my tragedy. He was offering his help but I was not ready to bear my soul yet. I was not ready to reveal my shame or pain. I did, however, tell him the details of the vision but without the context. I wanted to know his interpretation of it. He was highly educated, devout and one of the leaders in the Mosque. He was the one who interpreted the Imam's sermons and his other speeches from Arabic to English. Devoutly, he listened to me, and said, "I believe the key to the interpretation is to find out what the pix ax symbolizes. Find that; that's an important clue."

Meanwhile, the reverent, and devout leadership that the Imam brought to the Mosque would soon come to an end. When I went there one evening at the normal meeting time, the Imam was not there, and he was not at the Friday's service either. When I asked my friend where was he, he told me that he'd gone to a larger Mosque in another city, because this Mosque was too small to support him.

I was disappointed that he was no longer there. His sermons were inspirational to me and were rekindling in me a desire to preach again. I had often thought about talking to him about my problem but was reluctant to do so because of the language barrier. His leaving also had an impact on the Mosque. Attendance went down, and although they had good speakers at the Friday service, none measured up to the Imam's devoutness.

At any rate, the situation at home was not improving. My wife remained committed to her determination to get a divorce. My attorney advised me to sign the separation agreement instead of contesting it. The prospect of leaving our home under these circumstances was just unbearable.

Not only would it be another public humiliation, but an additional economic burden that I was not certain how I was going to bear. Becoming increasingly more frustrated as the court date neared, I told my attorney to respectfully tell the judge that I would violate his anticipated ruling, go to jail if necessary, and fast even until death or until the public became aware of my desperate plight. My desperation even sent me to a television station where I'd hoped to have my story aired, but that effort was to no avail.

At the weekly prayer meeting of my core group of church supporters, which took place three days before the court date, an unusual thing happened. Just before the close of the meeting, the chairman's niece, an avid supporter of mine, said these words in a quiet confident tone, "Reverend, the Lord has told me that it ain't gonna happen the way you think."

I gave the benediction, and the meeting was adjourned. The following day my wife came frantically from the front yard into the house where I was. She said wildly excited, "There's a big snake out in the front yard; please go out there and kill it." I went to the storage house and got a shovel, and told her to show it to me. She walked behind me and directed me to it. When I spotted it, I noticed that it was a long black snake stretched straight out in the grass near the highway. I slowly and quietly moved toward it with my shovel drawn back poised to strike it as soon as I got in striking distance. When I did I severed its head. I then picked it up with the shovel, with the intention of throwing it in the near by woods. When I did, I took a closer look. Surprisingly the snake was dead before I severed its head. It looked like a miniature version of the head of the serpent that I killed in my vision When I threw it in the woods nearby, a sudden thought landed in my mind, like a strange bird in the yard—*This thing that has come against you is dying.* But of course that night that thought was of no comfort to me. All night long, it seemed a thousand different demons tormented me. One, the demon of worry was the worse. It wouldn't let me sleep. Where would I stay? How would I pay rent and other expenses on just donations, which were uncertain at that? Those were just a few of my worries. And there was this, I loved my wife. I loved our home. And I loved my family. As I said earlier, one of my fundamental beliefs is the family. Take that away from me and I'm lost. When I thought about losing all of these, I felt like Samson must have felt when he realized that he'd lost all of his hair.

Naturally, the next morning, the court date, I got out of bed tired and depressed. Just before leaving the house to go to the courthouse, my wife embraced me, while crying, and said, "Chester, I love you, but we just can't stay together. I'm sorry." I shrugged her off and left.

When I arrived at the courthouse, I sat in a waiting room outside of the courtroom where our case would be heard. I waited for my lawyer to arrive. About fifteen minutes later my wife and her lawyer arrived. I watched them as they walked up the stairs; we were on the second floor. Some people took the elevator from the first floor to get to the second floor, while others walked up instead.

To see my wife of thirty years being escorted by another man whom she now had placed her trust, be it her lawyer, was astounding to me. It was as if I was having an out of body experience. She sat down on the front row of the waiting area, while I was seated on the back row. She did not look at me when she entered or when she sat. Even before she arrived as I sat in the waiting room, I prayed and made a decision to purge myself of all anger and resentment toward my wife, for anger can poison the spirit and become an impediment to clear thinking.

So I forgave her, accepted the reality of my condition and concentrated on what I would do after I left there. I also decided that I would not contest the separation agreement. My core group of very loyal supporters had started talking about their desire for me to get a building. Therefore, right there on the back bench in the courthouse, I felt a lifting of my spirit after I'd prayed and forgiven my wife.

Resigned to the fact now and no longer struggling against the inevitable, I got up from the back row and joined my wife. I spoke, and she in turn spoke to me and appeared to be happy that I'd joined her. She had a yellow notepad where I noticed she'd been writing her account of what she thought had taken place in our home. She was trying to prepare herself for her testimony before the judge. When she continued writing with me seated next to her, I noticed her hands shaking as she tried to write. It was then that I told her that I was not going to contest the separation agreement and that she no longer had to worry about testifying. I informed her that as soon as my attorney arrived I would tell him also what I'd decided to do. She was much relieved.

When my attorney arrived I told him my decision and he contacted her attorney. They arranged for the papers to be signed in an adjacent room. Before leaving, I asked my attorney what time did I have to be out of the house, and he said by twelve o'clock that night. I then left.

Upon leaving, I decided that the first thing that I would do was go get a hotel room, and just sleep until I was rested. Then I would make arrangements for a place to stay. But the hotel I went to was booked up for the weekend.

Consequently, I decided to go home and call a very dear beloved cousin of mine to see if I could rent a room there. Pride is one of the hardest things to swallow, but my cousin is a special soul; she's like a lily of the valley. She opened her heart and her home to me when I called, just as my own mother would have if she was still living.

Ironically enough, this is the cousin that introduced my father and mother to one another. Her wise father was the benevolent elder and leader of a large number of brothers and sisters of which my own father was the baby. I grew up hearing the stories of how her father and some of his brothers literally took care of my father, and sent him to school, because his mother, my grandmother, had died while he was still very young.

When my father would take us to visit his brother and my uncle, when we were very young, much of their conversation centered around my uncle's daughter who lived in New York at the time. Her parents were so proud of her and their conversation about her was so glamorous, that we children thought of her as a princess. In all of these years I've seen nothing in my cousin's character that would suggest to me that she's anything but a princess. Her home is also the place where my wife first stayed when I brought her to our hometown to introduce her to my mother when we were engaged to be married.

Other brothers and sisters lived there in their youth in order to attend a prominent high school near them. Our mother and father lived in another county so it was necessary to live in the county where the school was located if one wanted to attend that school. My mother and father were strong believers in education and whatever sacrifices were necessary for them to make to see that their children receive as much of it as possible, they made. Therefore my uncle's house played a central role in fulfilling my parents' educational dreams for their children. Because of all of this, my cousin's house was more than just a place to live, it was a historical and cultural landmark for our whole family.

It was while talking to my cousin on the phone that my wife walked in. When I finished the telephone conversation, she asked me who I was talking to. I told her who it was, and that I was going there to stay.

She objected. She said, "You don't have to go there to stay; this is just as much of your house as it is mine. Stay here until you get yourself an apartment."

I reminded her that we'd just signed a separation agreement and that I was supposed to be out of the house by twelve o'clock that night. Then I asked, "What are you going to tell the court when it finds out that I'm still in the house?"

She responded, "Those people don't tell me what to do."

I asked her again, "Are you sure?"

"Yes," she said.

I was ecstatic and started thinking that maybe the wife I married was returning back to me. I agreed to her proposition and told her that my cousin had insisted that I come over right then and see the room that she'd prepared for me.

Loraine said, "Go ahead and hurry up and come back so we can go out and get something to eat."

She was happy and excited that I'd decided to stay. When I stayed at my cousin's longer than I'd planned, I called her to tell her that I was on the way. She commented, "You're taking a mighty long time for somebody trying to reconcile."

We went out to eat when I got back and had a wonderful time. That Friday night our bedroom was a honeymoon suite. The next morning we got up and decided to spend the whole day at the beach. We took our own lunch, and a water cooler packed with snacks and refreshments.

On the way there, up the street from our home, we passed an exercise gym. My wife pointed it out to me as we passed and said, "That's where I go to exercise; I want you to go there with me. In one of my classes there are mostly men, and I don't feel comfortable being in there without you."

On Monday she enrolled me and handed me my enrollment card. This was the woman that I'd married. This was the one that

I was still in love with. However, on about the fifth day her joyful mood began to slowly fade like the sunshine amid the dark clouds of an approaching storm. Something vicious and demonic had taken leave of her for a few days, but it was now returning to possess her in order to attack me again.

It was then that I called my youngest brother, who by now had become one of my closest legal advisers and friends. This tragedy had brought us back to the close relationship of the days of our youth when I was his protector and guardian on the school playground. He always seemed to get in fights with boys much older and bigger than he was, and for fear of his safety, I'd always intervened and we'd both end up victorious. But his legal training and experience was now a library of wisdom that I often visited.

When I told him what had happened the past several days, he said, "That separation agreement has been violated!"

He then said, "Get off the phone right now, call your attorney, and let him know, before she calls the sheriff."

I couldn't reach my own attorney, but another attorney confirmed what my brother told me. I couldn't believe it. Later that night, that vicious thing had completely transformed my wife again, and she said to me in a violent state of anger, "Get out of here, right now, or I'll call the sheriff!"

I then went downstairs and called the sheriff department and told the deputy who answered the phone the situation. He said, "Reverend, we wouldn't come out there for nothing like that even if your wife did call; you all will have to go back before the judge again."

My wife was standing there listening, and when I hung up she went back upstairs frustrated. I took a big sigh of relief and felt that God had intervened.

CHAPTER 4

Wife's Deposition

A few weeks later, and approximately six months after our nightmare began, my civil attorney was now ready to depose the key persons involved in the litigation. Of course my wife was one of the central persons, or the key person, therefore, she was the first one he would depose.

However, the church attorney was also ready to take depositions. My wife was the first one on his list as well. In order to save time and money it was a mutual agreement by both attorneys to depose jointly.

The idea of being deposed was a cause of great concern to my wife. She was horrified by it. To me the thought of it was worse than swallowing castor oil, but I knew I had to swallow it, if the truth was to be uncovered. I also had hopes that perhaps it would help my wife, and that somehow its effect would be like an electrical shock that would jolt her mind back to reality.

As I sat across from her in the church attorney's office in the presence of the court reporter, and the three attorneys, I felt both anger and grief. I was angry that my own wife was testifying against me, and grieved that it was her illness causing her to do it. The following deposition under oath was her version of the events.

STATE OF NORTH CAROLINA   IN THE GENERAL COURT OF JUSTICE
                                     DISTRICT COURT DIVISION
COUNTY OF NEW HANOVER   02 CVD 0365

REV. CHESTER H. REDDRICK,
                    Plaintiff,   :   DEPOSITION OF:

                                     :
vs.   :   *LORAINE REDDRICK*

                                     :
MOUNT CALVARY MISSIONARY: '26 June 2002
BAPTIST CHURCH,   :
                    Defendant.   :

The deposition of LORAINE REDDRICK was conducted before Patti K. Holland, Court Reporter and Notary Public, in the offices of H. KENNETH STEPHENS, II, 701 Princess Street, Wilmington, North Carolina, commencing at 1:30 p.m. on Wednesday, June 26, 2002.

APPEARANCES

FOR THE PLAINTIFF: ROBERT J. HUME, III
                            604C Cedar Point Boulevard
                            Cedar Point, NC 28584

FOR THE DEFENDANT: H. KENNETH STEPHENS, II
                            Post Office Box 2237
                            Wilmington, North Carolina 28401

FOR THE DEPONENT: WILLIAM JOSEPH BONEY, JR.
                            406 Market Street
                            Wilmington, NC 28401

OTHER APPEARANCES: REVEREND CHESTER H. REDDRICK

PATTI K. HOLLAND, CCR
Post Office Box 4606
Wilmington, NC 28406
Telephone: (910) 686-9979

STIPULATIONS

1. That this deposition is being taken by Patti K. Holland, Court Reporter and Notary Public.
2. That the North Carolina Rules of Civil Procedure shall control the taking of said deposition and the use thereof in court.
3. Said deposition shall be taken for the purpose of discovery or for the use as evidence in the above entitled action, or for both purposes.
4. That all objections and motions to strike are reserved unto the respective parties except objections as to the form of the question. Said objections and motions to strike may be made at the time of the trial or any hearing of this cause and shall have the same force and effect as if made at the time of the taking of this deposition.
5. That the reading and signing of the transcript by the witness is waived.

LORAINE REDDRICK, being first duly sworn to tell the truth, the whole truth, and nothing but the truth, on her oath testified as follows:

DIRECT EXAMINATION

BY MR. STEPHENS TO MS. REDDRICK:

Q　Ms. Reddrick, I'm Kent Stephens, and I represent Mount Calvary Missionary Baptist church in a lawsuit filed by the Reverend filed here in New Hanover County with the file number of 02 CVD 0365. Have you ever had a deposition taken before?

A　No, I have not.

Q:　Just by way of introduction to the process you've been sworn and I have an opportunity to ask you some questions. Keep in mind that at any time if I ask you a questions you don't understand stop me and tell me you do not understand it. I'm not trying to trick you so don't worry about that because sometimes it may get confusing. If for any reason during the process you want to take a break for whatever reason just let us know and we'll do it. I don't think this is going to go that long, but even so if you wish to just let us know and we'll be glad to take a break.

I would ask that since we do have our court reporter if I ask you a question be sure to give a verbal response. By that I mean a lot of times in normal conversation you'll shake your head or go uh-huh, but be sure and make a verbal response so she'll be able to take it down.

I'll go ahead and get started with just some general questions sort of by way of a warmup. Like I say, remember to stop me if you don't understand or if you want me to rephrase the question.

First of all, would you state your name for the record.

A   Loraine Reddrick.
Q   Ms. Reddrick, where do you currently reside?
A   1801 Brierwood Road
Q   How long have you lived there?
A   Fifteen years.
Q   Are you employed, Ms. Reddrick?
A   Yes, I am.
Q   How are you employed?
A   With the New Hanover County School Board
Q   How? In what position?
A   Third grade teacher.
Q   Where do you teach?
A   Forest Hills School.
Q   How long have you been a teacher?
A   Thirty-three years.
Q   If you could tell me what you current marital status is.

A   We're in the process of filing for divorce. We have a—it's supposed to be a legal separation, but I think we have some problems with that.

Q   Are you married to the plaintiff in this action, Reverend Chester A. Frederick?

A   Yes.

Q   I'm just going to ask you generally are you aware of the lawsuit that Pastor Reddrick has filed against Mount Calvary Baptist Church?

A   Yes, I am aware of that.

Q   What is your understanding of the dispute between Pastor Reddrick and the church?

A   Yes, I am aware of that.

Q   What is your understanding of the dispute between Pastor Reddrick and the church?

A   That the officers in the church stated that I said something that I did not state and that he was wrongful dismissed.

Q   Going down a little bit further, what is it your understanding that the officers of the church said that you stated?

A   That I caught him in bed with his grandbaby's mother.

> BY MR. HUME: Could I ask you to speak up just a little tiny bit, Ms. Reddrick?
>
> BY WITNESS: Yes.
>
> BY MR. HUME: Could you repeat the last answer? please.

A   That I caught my husband in bed with his grandbaby's mother.

Q   Who would his grandbaby's mother be?

A   Nakia Brown.

Q   Did you make any statements in that regard to any of the deacons of Mount Calvary Baptist Church?

A   No. That I caught him in bed?

Q   Or did you make any statements regarding marital infidelity of your husband to them?

A   I made a statement of what I saw December the 7th as I entered the home.

Q   Who did you make that statement to?

A   George Vereen.

Q   As best you recall what did you tell Mr. Vereen?

A   December the 7th between 6:30 and 7:30 I drove up into my driveway and my husband was in the garage putting sheets and towels in the machine. When I walked in he looked at me and gave me the evil eye, and I went inside, and my grandson and his mother were sitting on the couch. She was sitting in the middle of the couch and he was on the right of her. I went in and I spoke to them. My grandson came over and he embraced me. When I spoke to each of them she said Huh. I wanted to state then to them his appearance as I entered the garage. I think he had an old baseball cap on. His hair was sweaty, and no socks on, some hard brown shoes, and some old pants, and a white shirt that he had preached in Sunday.

From there I entered the kitchen. There was clothing on the kitchen chair. I went upstairs to change clothes, my clothes, and my grandson followed me. As I got my clothes changed he came upstairs and sprawled out across the bed with arms and feet in the opposite direction and hand across the footboard of the bed. I stated to the deacon that from lady's intuition, patterns, behavior, and facts that I thought my husband had gone to bed with the baby's mother.

> BY MR. HUME: Could I ask you to repeat. Lady's intuition and something and something.

A   Facts, behavior, and patterns.

> BY MR. HUME: Thank you. I'm sorry.

Q   In your conversation with Deacon Vereen did you give him any more specifics than that about any facts that you based your assumption on?

A   Yes, I did.

Q   Could you tell me what else you told him.

A   I told him the facts were the conversation I had with my grandson and I had overheard the lady, the young lady, Nakia Brown, on the phone. Patterns that we had lived together for thirty years. The shirt, like putting on the shirt, and on the bed, sprawled across the bed. I also told him during that time that we had an argument about it. I asked him about it and he said if I said anything about it that he was going to tell everybody that I was insanely jealous. Then we went back and forth concerning that. Then he told me that he was going to tell the young lady to sue me for slandering her name.

And the third thing was that I tried to set him up so that I could get the house. And the fourth things was that I have lied about some things before, he had known me to lie about some things before.

In that conversation I had asked Deacon Vereen that this was totally confidential, that I was soliciting prayers. I had told him I had called the pastor of First Baptist Church, trying to get in touch with him to talk with him and I could not get in touch with him, but I was wondering who should I go to talk to because I felt like I needed someone to talk with. He said, he made the statement that he didn't know of anybody in the church that I could talk to, but he did give me the name, anybody he said, if I would recommend anybody it would be Janet Blue.

I also told him about the conversation I had with my grandson and what my grandson had stated, and that in the conversation he promised me that this would be totally confidential and he would not say anything to anyone about it if I didn't want him to say anything about it, that he would pray for the family.

Q   You said that you told Deacon Vereen about the conversations you've had with your grandson. What did you tell him about those conversations?

A   I told him that my grandson and I was going to get a sub sandwich and I wanted to know where was his granddaddy and momma when he was in the bathroom because my husband had told me that he had put something in the commode, and I also was missing four Prempro out of my package of pills. So I asked my grandson where were they, and he said they were in his room on his bed and wouldn't let him in.

Q You also stated that you overheard a phone call that Nakia Brown was engaged in that led you to believe that there was something going on between the two of them. Could you tell me about that phone call.

A I had come in from the gym one day and I heard him on the phone talking. From the way he was talking I thought it was one of the children. We have two sons. So I picked the phone up and I heard her on the phone on the other end, and she was crying, seemed to be, saying what were her parents and her family going to think of her when they found out what she had done.

Q In the part of the conversation that you heard did she say what she had done?

A She did not say what she had done.

Q Do you know whether or not if Deacon Vereen disclosed what you had told him?

A From my understanding the second Sunday in January I got a phone call, it was one of the ladies in the church, and asked me what was going on in the church, and said that Deacon Vereen had stated that I said that I had caught my husband in the bed with his grandbaby's mother.

Q Who was that lady that called you?

A Let me restate that. She did not tell me that this is what Deacon Vereen said, but I got up and went to the church to see. She asked me to go to the church to see what was going on. Deacon Vereen was doing such and so. And I got to the church and all the commotion, this is what I was told, and some of the ladies came by the house. You asked me what was the lady's name?

Q   Yes.

A   Annette Brown.

Q   She said that she wanted to know what was going on at the church?

A   Yes. She said that she had heard—I don't think she had gone to church. I don't know. I shouldn't say what I think. But anyway she had heard something was going on at the church and wanted to know did I know anything about it and for me to go out there and get my husband, was her words.

Q   Do you recall whether or not she said that Deacon Vereen had said anything or that something was just going on at the church?

A   There was something going on at the church.

Q   Why did you decide to confide in Deacon Vereen?

A   Well as I said before at the time I was desperate. I felt like I needed someone to talk to. He was a deacon in the church. I had called the church pastor where I was a member of before. I was trying to think of people in the church that I could go to talk to and so I decided to call Deacon Vereen and talk to him.

Q   You attended Mount Calvary Baptist Church, is that correct?

A   Yes.

Q   did you ever have occasion personally to hear Deacon Vereen mention or disclose what you said in front of other church members?

A   Have I heard him—

Q   Yes.

A   No.

Q   You're aware that there was a meeting of the congregation on January 17th where they voted on whether or not to terminate Pastor Reddrick.

A   Yes.

Q   Were you at that meeting?

A   No.

Q   Could you tell me who Janet Blue is.

A   She's a member of the church.

Q   Just one of the church leaders?

A   Yes.

Q   Did you confide in her what you felt—

A   No, I didn't.

Q   Did you right after December 7th of last year have a conversation with Deacon Nixon in which you disclosed any of this information?

A   Yes, I did.

BY MR. HUME: I'm sorry. What was the date?

A   No, I do not know the date.

Q   Do you know where it was?

A   Yes, I do.

Q   Where was that?

A   In the school cafeteria.

Q   That was at the Forest Hills School cafeteria.

A   The cafeteria.

Q   Could you tell me the best you recall what statements you made to Deacon Nixon at that time.

A   He came to me and said that he had his wife to call me, wanted to know how I was doing, so I kind of fell apart at that time and told him that I had came in December the 7th, the same thing that I had told Deacon Vereen, which I did not mention the baby, and the phone call, that type of thing. I did not go into any details. I just went into about the garage.

Q   Did you tell him generally what you suspected?

A   Well he would have to draw his own conclusion about that.

Q   Did you say that he had his wife call to ask how you were doing?

A   He told me that's what he was going to have his wife to call.

Q   Could you tell me how it came to be that you all had a conversation in the cafeteria.

A   His brother-in-law works at the school and he just came in, and he just came over to me, and I was with my children. It was lunchtime. I was standing there by the stage. We have a little platform there and I was standing by the stage and I was with my children at the time. He just came over and spoke. He always when he comes to the school he speaks to me.

Q   And just asked how you were doing.

A   Yes, and had his wife to call to see how I was doing.

Q   Was it you impression that before he talked to you that he had some specific knowledge that there was some problem you were having or was he just generally asking how you were doing?

A   You said my impression.

Q   Yes.

A   Well yes, he thought I was sick because I have been out of church.

Q   But you didn't have any reason to believe he suspected there was any problem between you and the pastor.

A   No.

Q   Were there any other adults in the cafeteria that day?

A   The maids. They're in there taking trash up from the tables, cleaning up the tables, the cafeteria staff.

Q   Do you think that anyone else in the cafeteria could have overheard your conversation?

A   I don't think so. I don't know. My table is at the end of the stage here and I'm with the children. They're collecting trays at other tables.

Q   I guess after the December 7th incident and you had these suspicions regarding your husband is there anyone else you confided in that you can recall?

A   My mother. She lives in Henderson, North Carolina.

Q   Anyone else in Wilmington that you can recall?

A   I can't recall besides the day that this incident happened, two ladies came by the incident at the church happened. Two ladies came by the house.

Q   Who were they?

A   Brenda Green and Edith Miller.

Q   When you say the incident at the church let me go back and ask you, what incident are you talking about?

A   That Sunday I went to the church to get him. He did not go in the pulpit.

BY MR. HUME: I'm sorry. I didn't hear the last two words.

A   He did not go into the pulpit

Q   That would have been the last Sunday that he actually attended a Sunday service of any sort as the pastor, is that correct?

A   Uh-huh (yes).

Q   Did you in fact go to church and take your husband away or get him to leave?

A   Yes. I went to the church and we left together, came home together.

Q   On that Sunday when you went to the church what did you observe happening at the church?

A   When I entered the church ground on the little breezeway I came in and I went into the back of the church, the front of the church. I went in and I asked where he was and someone said he was in the study. Not study, sorry. In the fellowship hall. So I started to the fellowship hall. I saw a couple of the deacons as I was on the way to the fellowship hall. I just went back in the office where he was and he was back there. He was back in the office at the time.

Q   Did you just say he needed to leave and he left or was he having a confrontation with anyone? Do you know?

A   No, he was not having a confrontation. Rena Lennon, the church clerk, I believe she was giving him a letter at the time. So I just told him, I said, "Let's go home."

Q   Did you have any conversations with Deacon Vereen at that time?

A   No, I didn't.

Q   This is when you went to the church as a result of Annette Brown calling you?

A   Pardon me?

Q   You went to the church as a result of Ms. Brown, Annette Brown, calling you.

A   Yes.

Q   Ms. Reddrick, in the domestic lawsuit in the Complaint that you filed you alleged that the Pastor Reddrick had engaged in marital misconduct. Is the incident on the 7th and a relationship with Ms. Brown what you were describing in that Complaint?

A   Yes.

Q   Would Ms. Brown be the individual that in your Complaint you said that you would name at the trial of the matter?

A   Yes.

Q   You also allege in your Complaint that the pastor has accused you of being mentally ill.

A   Yes.

Q   Could you describe when he has done that.

A   He told the children, told my mother, he told the people at the church that I was delusional. When we had decided that we were going to make this work, get some counseling, we would make it work, and so we went to a psychiatrist together. From that report he would just tell everybody that I'm delusional and he has said that he's going to tell everybody I'm insanely jealous and delusional.

Q   Is it safe to say that word of the problems between you and the pastor and the allegations regarding Ms. Brown became spread throughout the community?

A   Yes.

Q   Can you tell me, if you remember, when you recall first becoming aware that these allegations were out in the community?

A   I think that Sunday I went—that was my first time, when I went over to the church to get him.

Q   Up until that Sunday, which was his last Sunday in the church, you weren't aware that there were rumors of this out in the community.

A   No. I don't recall. That was the first time.

Q   Just a couple of more questions, Ms. Reddrick. When you spoke with Deacon Nixon at Forest Hills was there any particular reason that you confided in him?

A   Well I told him that I was going to call Deacon Vereen, and at the time when he came over and he was concerned about I had been ill, and so I just—

Q   Did you confide in him at that time because he was a deacon or because he was a friend or can you tell me exactly why you would have confided in him at that time?

A   Because he was a deacon and my husband had said go to the deacons, talk to the deacons, when I was talking about I needed someone to talk to.

Q   Your husband had told you to talk to the deacons as a result of this incident?

A   Before this happened that's what he told me.

BY MR. STEPHENS: I don't have any further questions.

CROSS EXAMINATION

BY MR. HUME TO MS. REDDRICK:

Q   I just have a few questions, Ms. Reddrick. Currently are you on any medication?

A   Yes. I'm on Prempro.

Q   What is Prempro?

A   Estrogen.

Q   That's replacement of the hormone estrogen as menopause occurs or is about to occur, is that correct?

A   Yes.

Q   How old is Nakia Brown?

A   Twenty-five I guess. I don't know. I think about twenty-five.

Q   Nakia Brown had at the time of this incident how many children?

A   Two.

Q   What were their ages?

A   I don't know. I know the oldest one because that's my son's. He's five.

Q   hat is that child's name please, the five year old?

A   Malieck.

Q   How do you spell Milieck please.

A   M-a-l-I-e-c-k.

Q   What's his last name?

A   Brown.

Q   Are you talking any drugs at all like Xanax or Paxil?

A   No. I have a statement from my medical doctor because he said that that's what caused me to be like I am, the Prempro, and I have a statement from my doctor that my medication had nothing to do with—

Q   I'm confused. Your doctor said—

A   I have a statement from my medical doctor saying that the Prempro and I take some medication for acid reflux has nothing to do.

Q   Do you have that with you by any chance?

A   Yes, I do.

Q   Would you be kind enough to show it to me.

        (Witenss produces document.)

Q   So if I read this correctly you were examined by Dr. Howard Grotsky, psychologist.

A   Yes.

Q   At the Human Growth and Training Associates.

A   Yes.

Q   How did you come to be examined by him at that particular business or practice or whatever the appropriate designation is?

BY MR. BONEY: I'm going to object to this. I don't think this has any relevance to the issue at hand here. I don't mind you looking at those things, but they're not part of the record in this file. You can subpoena them. She is not here under a subpoena to produce documents, and in an effort to just speed this up I don't mind you looking at those documents, but they are medical and legal privileged documents.

BY WITNESS: Does he know the reason for those documents? Because he had called me crazy.

Q   Based on previous answers you believe that there is no medication you are taking that would in any way affect your capacity to testify accurately and truthfully today, is that correct?

A   That's true.

Q   My comments will relate specifically to what you told Deacon Vereen rather than what you saw or heard yourself. Do you understand the distinction there?

A   Uh-huh (yes).

Q   That's what I'm going to limit this to and make sure that I understand completely what it was that you told Deacon Vereen. First of all, when you spoke to Deacon Vereen can you give us a date for that by any chance?

A   December the 21st.

Q   Is that an about date or are you sure of the date?

A   I'm sure.

Q   What allows you to be sure of the date?

A   Because I was on Christmas vacation.

Q   But weren't you on vacation more than one day?

A   It was the beginning of Christmas vacation.

Q   The very first day of Christmas vacation?

A   Yes, because it was a work day, but I did not work.

Q   What did you tell Deacon Vereen before you related any details of what you saw on December 7th? What did you say to him as well you can the exact words that you used to him?

A   Before I went into details?

Q   Yes.

A   Like with the incident that happened?

Q   In other words, what was the beginning of the conversation? What did you say to him before you related what you had seen on December 7th?

A   I told him I needed someone to talk with and I wanted to talk with him.

Q   How did he respond when you said that?

A   Sure, anything, Ms. Reddrick.

Q   Did you then say that you wanted everything said to him to be held in complete confidence?

A   Yes, I asked him.

Q   So you asked him would he keep it.

Q   Yes.

Q   You didn't simply state you wanted it—

A   Yes, I told him. I told him at the end, yes.

Q   At the end.

A   Yes, at the end.

Q   So at the end—

A   I told him, yes.

Q   That you wanted this conversation to be held confidential.

A   Uh-huh (yes).

Q   What was his response to that?

A   He would keep it confidential. Okay, Ms. Reddrick.

Q   Okay, Ms. Reddrick.

A   Yes. If you don't want me to say anything I won't.

Q   As I understand your testimony—and if I'm wrong, I'm not a very good transcriber, I don't write terribly quickly, so If I've missed something you're going to correct me, right? What I understood from your testimony is that you told Deacon Vereen that on December 7th you returned to your home that you did share with your husband, Reverend Reddrick, between 6:30 and 7:30 p.m., is that correct?

A   Yes, about that time.

Q   You drove up in the driveway of the home and you said you saw your husband in the garage. Where is the garage in relationship to the driveway? In other words, is there a driveway whereby you can pull from the driveway directly into the garage?

A   Yes.

Q   Did you in fact pull the car into the garage or leave it outside?

A   No, I left it outside.

Q   Was there any reason for that at that particular moment?

A   I can't remember.

Q   What I'm asking, is there enough room for you to park the car in the garage while someone is using the washing machine?

A   I think so. The bike was in the garage. The child's bike was in the garage.

Q   So that may have been some impediment to pulling the car in.

A   Yes.

Q   You told Deacon Vereen that you saw your husband putting sheets and towels in the washing machine, is that correct?

A   Uh-huh (yes).

Q   Did you tell the deacon that you had in any way examined these sheets and towels that he was putting in the washing machine?

A   No, I didn't.

Q   You told Deacon Vereen that your husband gave you the evil eye.

A   Yes.

Q   What did that mean, Ms. Reddrick.

A   He looked at me and rolled his eyes at me.

Q   He looked at you—

A   He looked at me and rolled his eyes at me.

Q   Did Deacon Vereen ask you when you mentioned the evil eye what you meant by what was the evil eye?

A   No, he didn't.

Q   So he didn't inquire at all about what the evil eye meant.

A   No.

Q   You told Deacon Vereen that—Is it Nokia, N-o-k-i-a?

A   I believe k-i-a, yes. I believe so.

Q   N-o-k-i-a?

A   N-a.

Q   N-a.

A   I believe.

Q   You told Deacon Vereen that you found Nakia sitting on the couch with her son, Milieck, right?

A   Yes.

Q   Did you give Deacon Vereen any other details about their appearance sitting on the couch?

A   No, I didn't.

Q   you told Deacon Vereen how your husband was dressed, did you not?

A   Yes.

Q   How did you describe your husband as being dressed to Deacon Vereen?

A   I stated that before.

Q   I'm asking you the same question again.

A   His hair was sweaty. He had a white shirt on he had preached in Sunday. He didn't have on any socks. He had on brown hard shoes and some old pants on.

Q   Hard shoes. Is that the phrase you used, hard shoes?

A   Yes, hard shoes.

Q   Does that mean like leather shoes?

A   Yes, leather, hard shoes that had gotten wet and looked like it was just hard.

Q   You said you saw some clothing on the kitchen chair.

A   Yes.

Q   Did you tell Deacon Vereen what that clothing was?

A   No, I didn't.

Q   You said you went upstairs to change, is that correct?

A   Yes.

Q   And your husband was lying on the bed.

A   No. I said as I was changing when he came up.

Q   As you were changing.

A   When I was changing he came up.

Q   You said, quote, sprawled across the bed.

A   Yes.

Q   Did you describe anything else to Deacon Vereen about his appearance on the bed?

A   The same thing I just said. That's all.

Q   Other than the sprawling part did you describe anything else about him on the bed?

A   Like I stated before arms and legs in opposite direction, legs across the bed, the footboard.

Q   Anything else about his appearance or activity at that time?

A   No.

Q   That you discussed with Deacon Vereen.

A   Not that I recall.

Q   You mentioned that based on the facts—you mentioned the word facts, behavior, and patterns. Those were the three words that you used in your direct testimony. Did Deacon Vereen question you on what you meant by facts, behavior, and patterns?

A   No.

Q   Did Deacon Vereen ask you to explain what you meant by lady's intuition when you used that?

A   No, but I did say we had been married thirty years. He did not need to explain to him things.

Q   You described a conversation with your grandson. Did you give to Deacon Vereen the contents in any way of the conversation that you had with your grandson?

A   No.

Q   To the best of your recollection please tell us what that conversation was only as you related it to Deacon Vereen. I realize there may be details that you got from your grandson that you didn't tell Deacon Vereen. I'm just asking you to tell me here today to the best of your recollection what did you tell Deacon Vereen your grandson and you said back and forth?

A   I don't know exactly what I told Deacon Vereen.

Q   Just do your best.

A   But all I know what my grandson told me, but I do not know like exact words I told Deacon Vereen concerning what my grandson said.

Q   Just do your best. Okay?

A   I told Deacon Vereen that when I asked my grandson where was his granddaddy and momma while he was in the bathroom and he said in my room on my bed and wouldn't let me come in. I peeped through the door.

Q   Is that it? I'm not suggesting there is more. I'm just asking is that it.

A   I don't know exactly what I did tell him, but he said he heard up and down noise, he heard some up and down noise.

Q   What kind of noise?

A   He described it as up and down noise.

Q   So he was telling you that the door was opened.

A   Closed.

Q   I thought you said he peeped in.

A   The door was closed and he said he peeped through the door.

Q   Peeped through the door. Was there a key hole in the door?

A   What I assumed he was saying—

Q   Well just answer my question if you would first. Is there a key hold in the door?

A   No.

Q   We'll get into that another time. I guess we'll hold that for the divorce case. So did you tell Reverend Vereen to the best of your knowledge the child peeped through the door?

A   Yes, that's the word I used. These are his words. I peeped. You asked me what did I tell Deacon Vereen that the child said. The child said I peeped through the door. So these are his words.

Q   Did Deacon Vereen inquire as to the age of Malieck?

A   No, he didn't.

Q   Do you have any reason to think that Deacon Vereen knows the age of Malieck?

A   He's seen Malieck.

Q Has he met Malieck?

A Yes.

Q He's been introduced to him? He would know who he was?

A He had seen him at the church. Malieck had been to the church.

Q Did you give him the name of this boy you talked to when you described what you described before?

A I didn't give him a name, no.

Q You didn't give him the name.

A No.

Q So how did he know this was Malieck if you didn't give him Malieck's name.

A I said my grandson.

Q But you have more that one grandchild, don't you?

A No.

Q I thought you said before you have two grandchildren.

A I did not say that.

Q You have only one grandchild then, Malieck.

A I said the mother has two children.

Q I'm sorry. Forgive me. I got confused there. The other child was not your grandchild.

A True.

Q Did Deacon Vereen ever have a conversation with Malieck?

A I don't know if he has had a conversation with Malieck.

Q Let me put it this way. Did he ever have a conversation in your presence?

A He may have spoke to Malieck like around the church to speak to him.

Q To say hello.

A Hello, yes.

Q In your presence did he ever have a conversation with Maieck?

A I can't recall.

Q Did he inquire of you whether or not he regarding Malieck as a reliable witness, a kid that knew the difference between fantasy and reality?

A No.

Q   Now there came a time when you argued with your husband and he said he would tell people you are insanely jealous if you told people your suspicions, is that correct?

A   Yes.

Q   Did you relate that to Deacon Vereen?

A   Yes.

Q   Would you describe yourself as a jealous person?

A   No.

Q   I heard you say and not clearly that you mentioned something about, quote, unquote, trying to set him up. Did I hear correctly?

A   Yes.

Q   And this is something that you told to Deacon Vereen.

A   Yes.

Q   Did you say more than that, trying to set him up?

A   That's all I said.

Q   You said no more than that.

A   That's what I said.

Q   For instance you didn't say that you had tried to set him up and you had had some results from trying to set him up.

A   No. That's all I said.

Q   Did you tell him when the attempt to, quote, set him up occurred?

A   No.

Q   He didn't ask you that?

A   No.

Q   Did Deacon Vereen ask you to elaborate on one single detail of what you related to him?

A   No.

Q   So he just heard the information and just said nothing.

A   He didn't ask me to elaborate, no.

Q   He did not. Okay. You said that you told the deacon that you had lied about things before.

A   I didn't. I told the deacon that he told me, my husband told me I had lied before then about things before.

Q   You told Deacon Vereen that your husband had said that you had lied about things before.

A   Yes.

Q   Is that in fact true?

A   No.

Q   Would you describe to us as best you can approximately how long you spoke to Deacon Vereen on what you describe as the 21st of December.

A   I don't remember.

Q   I'm not suggesting that you can say ten minutes and twelve seconds. What I'm asking you is do the best estimating. Do you think it was three minutes or half an hour?

A   Between a half hour. About half an hour.

Q   During this time did Deacon Vereen take any notes?

A   No.

Q   Did he ask you to repeat anything that you had said so that he could make sure he understood it correctly?

A   Not that I recall.

Q   Did you tell Deacon Vereen that four Prempro pills were missing?

A   Yes.

Q   And he did not inquire as to what a Prempro pill was?

A   No.

Q   Do you have any idea if he know what that pill is one way or the other?

A   No.

Q   You described to him the overheard phone call, did you not?

A   Yes.

Q   Did Deacon Vereen ask you—

A   No, because he just looked—he didn't say anything.

Q   So when Nakia made a reference to having done something Reverend Vereen didn't ask you if you knew what in fact she was referring to.

A   No.

Q   There came a time when you found out that your husband was not allowed to preach on the second Sunday in January, is that correct?

A   Yes.

Q   Have you subsequently learned that there was a meeting that was held at which a vote was taken to in fact fire your husband?

A   I heard.

Q   But you had no knowledge of that meeting before it occurred, is that correct?

A   I can't recall that. Someone called to the house and said they was having a meeting.

Q   Did they tell you what the meeting was?

A   No.

Q   Certainly Deacon Vereen didn't call you and tell you there was a meeting, did he?

A   No. A lady called me and was calling my husband.

Q   Thank you for the correction. I appreciate that. How did you come to learn that Deacon Vereen has told people not what you told him but rather that you told him that you caught your husband in bed with Nakia? From whom did you learn that he was saying that you had said that when in fact you had not said it, if you remember?

A   I think that Sunday.

Q   Do you recall from whom you heard the representation of what Deacon Vereen had said? Can you recall?

A   I'm not sure, but I think it was those two ladies.

Q   You mentioned that you had a discussion with Deacon Nixon. Can you tell us as best you can when that occurred in the cafeteria. When was that?

A   I don't know the date.

Q   Was it after Christmas vacation was over since you were in the school cafeteria? May I reasonably assume that's the case?

A   It was before.

Q   Before Christmas?

A   Yes, before Christmas vacation.

Q   So you spoke to Nixon before you spoke to Vereen.

A   Yes.

Q   If my notes are correct you didn't go into great detail with Nixon.

A   No.

Q   But you did mention a few of the things that you had seen in the garage, is that right?

A   Yes.

Q   When did you confide in your mother your suspicions in relationship to the brief conversation with Nixon and then the more elaborate conversation with Vereen?

A   After he had called my son and told my son I was insane and my son called my mother. My son called my mother. My mother called me to let me know my son was upset.

Q   What is the name of the church clerk who gave the letter to your husband?

A   Rena Lennon.

Q   Did you subsequently come to understand that that letter said he was terminated as pastor of the church?

A   No, that letter didn't.

Q   Did you subsequently come to learn that that's what the letter said that was handed to him at that time?

A   No.

Q   What did the letter say, if you know?

A   I can't tell you exact words.

Q   What was the import? The import of the letter was what?

A   About the accusation. Until the accusation was cleared up or something. I don't know.

Q   I didn't hear something terribly well. Is it your previous testimony today that you husband told you to speak to the deacons about your problems?

A   Yes.

Q   What were his exact words, if you can recall?

A   We had an argument and he said to go talk to the deacons, they can't do anything to me.

    BY MR. STEPHENS: Would you repeat that last part.

A   Go talk to the deacons, they can't do anything to me.

Q   Does you mother have any contact to your knowledge with anyone at your church?

A   No. My mother lives in Henderson.

Q   To your knowledge she has no friends in the church, someone that she would call and talk about this. Okay. So excluding your mother the only two other people that you have described anything about this incident to were Deacon Nixon in a very quick conversation before Christmas vacation started and Deacon Vereen, a more lengthy conversation on December 21st, is that correct?

A   Restate that question.

Q   For the sake of this question we're excluding your mother. Did you speak to anyone else before your husband was suspended as pastor, anyone else, about the details of your suspicions other than Deacon Nixon and Vereen?

A   Yes.

Q   Who else?

A   I talked to an attorney.

Q   Other than the attorney?

A   Not that I can recall.

Q   Do you have any reason to think that attorney violated the confidence of that conversation with him or her?

A   No.

BY MR. HUME: Give me two minutes with my client to see if there's something that I'm missing.

(OFF RECORD—SHORT BREAK)
(BACK ON RECORD)

Q   (Mr. Hume continues to witness.) Ms. Reddrick do you know any reason why Deacon Vereen would have a grudge against your husband?

A   I can't answer that. I don't know.

Q   Do you know of any reason why he would?

A   I couldn't answer that.

Q   Do you know of any grudge he has?

A   No.

Q   Do you believe that nevertheless Deacon Vereen is using what you said and distorting what you said to get at your husband?

A   Now I believe that. I believe that, yes.

Q   Final question. Just so the record is remarkably redundant, you have at no time told any human being that you caught your husband in bed with the mother of your grandson.

A   I have not told anyone that I caught my husband in the bed with his grandson's mother.

Q   Is it also true that you have told no one that you have direct evidence of that, merely suspicions of his sleeping with his grandson's mother? Is that question clear? I can rephrase it.

A   Pardon me?

Q   Let me rephrase it. Is it also not clear that you have not told anyone that you have any hard evidence that your husband had sex with the mother of your grandson?

BY MR. BONEY: I'm going to object to that question because I don't understand it. You said is it not clear that you have no evidence.

Q   Have you ever told anyone that you actually know that your husband slept with the mother of your grandson?

A   Have I told—

Q   Anyone that you actually know that to be a fact.

A   No. Based on the evidence that—no, I have not told anybody I know.

Q   Your husband's alleged infidelity is merely a suspicion, correct?

A   Well the facts and evidence, what I have, yes.

Q   It's merely a suspicion.

A   From the facts and evidence that I have. From the facts and evidence. This is what I'm basing it on.

Q   That is a suspicion rather than actual knowledge.

A   From the facts and evidence that I've said today that that's what I'm basing it on.

Q   Is there anything that you left out of what counsel for the church has gone over and I've gone over, is there any fact that you've left out that would be a, quote, unquote, fact establishing the infidelity of your husband?

> BY MR. BONEY: That was not the question she was asked. She was asked what she told Deacon Vereen. She was not asked the question that you're asking.

> BY MR. HUME: All right. I'll withdraw that. I understand your objections. Nothing further at this time.

REDIRECT EXAMINATION

BY MR. STEPHENS TO MS. REDDRICK:

Q   I've got just a couple and I don't mean to repeat but I'm not sure if I caught a couple of things. You mentioned two ladies who came to your house I believe after the Sunday where the pastor was removed from the church, is that correct?

A   Yes.

Q   Who were those two ladies?

A   Brenda Green and Edith Miller.

Q   Did they say to you that Deacon Vereen said that you had alleged your husband had been sleeping with Nakia Brown?

A   I'm not sure of their exact words, but they came in "is it true". This is what they were saying.

Q   They were asking you was it true whether or not your husband was sleeping with Nakia Brown?

A   Yes.

Q   But you don't recall them saying Deacon Vereen said that at church or anywhere else?

A   No.

Q   Do you recall whether or not they said or indicated to you that those allegations were circulating at the church?

A   Repeat that now.

Q   Do you recall whether or not that they indicated to you that those allegations about your husband were circulating among the church members that day?

A   They asked me is it true. They came in, "All we want to know, is it true, did you catch your husband in the bed?

Q   And they never said that they heard that from Deacon Vereen.

A   No. They didn't tell me that that day.

Q   Did they ever tell you that?

A   (Witness nods.)

Q   Do you have any personal knowledge that Deacon Vereen ever told anyone else?

A   No. From my husband. My husband came in and said Deacon Vereen told him.

Q   When what that?

A   I can't remember.

Q   Do you recall whether or not that was after a meeting with the deacons?

A   No.

Q   Do you know when that meeting took place?

A   No. I don't know exact dates of when it took place.

Q   The second Sunday in January when you went to the church to pick up your husband you had been called by Ms. Annette Brown to go to church, is that correct?

A   She called me and wanting to ask me what was going on out there, that I needed to go get my husband.

Q   Why did she tell you that you needed to go get him?

A   She just said you need to go get him. Go on out there. Go see what is wrong with your husband. Go get him.

Q   Did she say there was something wrong with your husband?

A   Those are her words. She said there was something going on at the church and I needed to go get my husband.

Q   You went to the church and asked him to leave with you, is that correct?

A   Well I went to the church and I found him. I just said when he finished up what he was doing let's go.

Q   Do you know whether or not that Sunday your husband had attempted to address these allegations with the church body or the congregation?

A   No, I do not know.

Q   Did he indicate to you that that's what he wanted to do that day?

A   I heard that's what he did.

Q   Who did you hear that from?

A   I don't know who it was, but I just heard that.

Q   You didn't hear that the deacons, or Deacon Vereen specifically, were airing these allegations before the congregation, did you?

A   No.

Q   So it's your understanding that it was your husband who wanted to address congregation with these issues, is that correct?

A   Yes, that's correct.

BY MR. STEPHENS: I've got nothing further.

RECROSS EXAMINATION

BY MR. HUME TO MS. REDDRICK:

Q   One follow-up. The ladies who came to see you asking you is it true that you caught your husband in bed with a woman, what did you say?

A   No.

BY MR. HUME: Thank you. Nothing further.

(WHEREUPON, the deposition was concluded CROSS EXAMINATIONat 2:50 p.m.)

(46

STATE OF NORTH CAROLINA

COUNTY OF NEW HANOVER

<u>CERTIFICATE</u>

I, Patti K. Holland, a Notary Public and Court Reporter in and for the State of North Carolina, County of New Hanover, do hereby certify that the foregoing forty-five (45) pages constitute a true and accurate transcript of the testimony of LORAINE REDDRICK, which was taken down and transcribed by me on the date set forth in the record and before the persons named therein; further, that the witness was duly sworn by me before the taking of testimony. I further certify that I am not a relative, employee, attorney or counsel of any of the parties, nor am I a relative or employee of such attorney or counsel, nor am I financially interested in this action.

WITNESS my hand and notarial seal this the 1st day of July, 2002.

_____ (SEAL)
Patti K. Holland

My Commission Expires:

    May 12, 2007

After the deposition was over, my wife and I went out for dinner. I was hesitant about initiating the conversation with her about her presentation. She seemed reserved and disappointed, like a baseball player returning to the dug out after a strike out. I was praying that perhaps she was reconsidering her beliefs, and that the mental shock that I'd hope for had actually happened.

Unable to wait any longer, I decided to test the waters. I kindly asked her how she thought she had done. To my surprise, she said her lawyer thought that she'd talked too much. That statement and her sense of resignation concurred with my own opinion, and the opinion of my attorney, that my wife's beliefs were just opinions in her mind. Although to her, they were more than just opinions, but were fact based on what she believed to be truth.

Of course this is why the psychiatrist called her condition delusional. Feeling encouraged that she shared with me what I considered to be negative information about herself, from her own attorney, fueled my hopes. Maybe a break through was taking place. I continued the appraisal, although doing so very carefully, so as not to offend her. I especially wanted to know if she was resigned now to the fact that her beliefs were just opinions, as she'd stated in the deposition and no longer facts, as she'd contended before. That question touched a raw nerve, and she said angrily that she'd never agreed to that. That window of fresh air that had been briefly open at our dinner table was now closed, and we spent the rest of the evening with me trying to put salve on a wound that was not healing.

My wife returned to her old ways, and even chastised me for not coming to her defense while my attorney was deposing her. She said that if I were a man I would have stopped him; therefore, she said she could no longer live with a man like me. Her long withdrawals in her room now, when she came home from work, and her unyielding bitterness toward me became permanent fixtures in our relationship like the pictures on the walls in our home.

Meanwhile, the call for a building by some of the members in my core group of supporters was finally answered. They were growing tired of the home meetings. They wanted a meeting place of their own at least until the lawsuit was over. There was some optimistic talk from some of them that even more people would join us if we had a building but I did not share that same opinion.

Six months had now passed and the scandal had taken its toll. Most people had already made up their minds, I reasoned. Therefore, it was my opinion that our core group was probably the extent of what could be expected. I told them that in order to shield them from any disappointment.

However, I had some reservations about getting a building. I was concerned about the expense. And not only that, although I needed the support of these dear souls, I was a changed person. Would they accept these changes in me? That too was a concern of mine.

I no longer believed in some things I used to believe. This tragedy had reinforced my long held conviction that most people in the traditional mainstream churches that I'd been affiliated with most of my life are not governed by the Word of God!

My refuge in the mosque also impacted my belief. I no longer believed that a choir and musician were necessary for true worship. Based on my experience, I now realized that all of that emphasis and time placed on who will play, who will lead the solo, and what robes to wear, detract the people from true worship. I also now believed that the wearing of expensive clothes was not necessary for true worship, and that the emphasis should not be on what one has on but on whom one is worshipping.

A lot of other things that I used to think were necessary for worship now seemed foolish and insignificant to me. My belief in God, was never at issue in my crisis. In fact it was stronger now than ever. I was convinced that in the vision, God was showing me the beginning and the ending of my trial. What I struggled with now was, what was God's will for me in light of this experience.

What was the meaning and purpose of this? After much prayer and soul searching the answer came. I found it in St. John the fourth chapter, verses five through twenty four, especially verses twenty three and twenty four, where Jesus himself says to the Samaritan woman,

"But the hour cometh, and now is when the true worshipers shall worship the father in spirit and in truth: for the father seeketh such to worship him. God is a spirit; and they that worship him must worship him in spirit and in truth."

I believe that with all of my heart. To worship anything else is only idolatry. To worship one's self, one's culture, one's race, one's traditions, and one's nation instead of God in spirit and in truth, is one of the greatest delusions plaguing mankind.

Therefore on our first Sunday worship, Saint John the fourth chapter was the sermon's text for the morning. It would also become the scriptural foundation for what I called The Village Worship Center. Even though there was no musician or choir—we couldn't afford one even if we wanted one—everyone was amazed, including myself, that the power and glory of God filled the house.

One worshiper said afterwards, "Reverend, the anointing of God is still on you." I had not preached in six months and I'm sure that some of my loyal supporters wondered if the hand of God was still on me.

CHAPTER 5

The Two Deacons' Depositions

Then, exactly fifty days after my wife's deposition, and well over six months now since that deacon's meeting occurred on January 8, when the chairman confronted me with the allegation, the time finally arrived for him to be deposed.

My attorney decided to depose him and another one of the deacons on the same day. The other was Deacon Canty, the one who according to the private investigator's report visited some of the members' homes, spreading the rumor and soliciting them to vote against me at the meeting on January 17th based on the slanderous falsehood that he was spreading.

I assumed that they were now aware of the fact that my wife had already been deposed.

Furthermore, I assumed that they were now aware of her sworn testimony. My assumption was based on the fact that their own lawyer was one of the attorney's that deposed her. Therefore, I was more than curious to hear what the chairman would say now about the conversation my wife had with him on the twenty first of December, in light of her sworn testimony, which contradicted his.

I was more than curious to hear how he would explain some other matters as well. For example, how would he explain the violation of the written agreement, which called for me to step down from the pulpit with pay until the accusation against me had been resolved? How would he explain not responding to my attorney's written request for information concerning the nature of the January 17th meeting? How would he explain his refusal to abide by the association's ruling when they nullified the meeting, even though they were the same one's who presided at the meeting. How could they be right in one instance and wrong in the other? And finally, how would he explain that the church didn't have any bylaws when they were in the new member's booklet and taught in the church by the new members committee for years?

The following depositions would answer those questions and more.

STATE OF NORTH CAROLINA

COUNTY OF NEW HANOVER

IN THE GENERAL COURT OF JUSTICE
DISTRICT COURT DIVISION
01 CVD 0365

REV. CHESTER H. REDDRICK,)
)
               Plaintiff,)
)
vs.   )
)
MOUNT CALVARY MISSIONARY   )
BAPTIST CHURCH,   )
)
               Defendant.)
_____)

DEPOSITION OF GEORGE VEEREEN

DATE: August 15, 2002

TIME: 10:45 a.m. o'clock

PLACE: Law Offices of H. Kenneth Stephens, II Wilmington, North Carolina

INDEX

EXHIBITS:

Plaintiff's Exhibit 1: Handbook for New Members
Plaintiff's Exhibit 2: Church Covenant
Plaintiff's Exhibit 3: January 13, 2002 letter
Plaintiff's Exhibit 4: January 24, 2002 letter
Plaintiff's Exhibit 5: January 15, 2002 letter

APPEARANCES

For the Plaintiff: Robert J. Hume, III, Esquire
                     604-C Cedar Point Boulevard
                     Cedar Point, NC 28584

For the Defendant: H. Kenneth Stephens, II, Esquire
                     P.O. Box 2237
                     Wilmington, NC 28402

STIPULATIONS

It is hereby stipulated and agreed between the parties to this action, through their respective counsel of record:

1. The Deposition of GEORGE VEEREEN, shall be taken on August 15, 2002, beginning at 10:45 a.m. in the law offices of H. Kenneth Stephens, II, Wilmington, North Carolina.

2. Said Deposition shall be taken for the purpose of discovery or for use as evidence in the above entitled action, or for both purposes.

3. Any objections of any party hereto as to notice of taking of said Deposition or as to the time or place thereof, or as to the competency of the person before whom the same shall be taken are deemed to have been met.

4. Objections to questions and motions to strike answers need not be made during the taking of this Deposition but may be made for the first time during the progress of the trial of this case, or at any pretrial hearing held before any judge for the purpose of ruling thereon, or at any other hearing of said case at which said Deposition might be used, except that and objection as to the form of a question must be made at the time such question is asked or objection is waived as to the form of the question.

5. Rules of the North Carolina Rules of Civil Procedure shall control the taking of said Deposition and the use thereof in court.

6. Except as waived by this stipulation, the provisions of the North Carolina Rules of Civil Procedure shall apply to the taking of said Deposition and as to their submission to the respective deponent, certification and filing, except that notice of filing is hereby given.

7. It is stipulated and agreed between the parties hereto that Frances Y. Grice shall be Commissioner for the purpose of taking this Deposition.

8. It is further stipulated that the signature of the witness to the Deposition is waived.

GEORGE VEEREEN, being first duly sworn to tell the truth, the whole truth and nothing but the truth, on his oath, testified as follows:

DIRECT EXAMINATION

BY MR. HUME:

Q: Good morning, Mr. Veereen, my name is Robert Hume and I'm the attorney for Reverend Reddrick. You understand that, right? Don't you?

A: Oh, yes.

Q: Okay. And, the purpose of this meeting here today is what's called a pretrial deposition. I'm going to ask you questions. The purpose of this deposition is to elicit answers under oath from you, Mr. Veereen, and these answers can be used later on at trial. And, I'm going to do my best to ask questions that are clear and concise. And It's your right, and indeed I would say really your obligation, if my question is unclear to tell me that. I'm not here trying to trick you, I'm just trying to find out what you know and what you don't know.

A: Okay.

Q: Fair enough? So, at any time you want to take a break you can do so. At any time you want to have a little rest you can do so, but I would ask you to finish whatever question you're answering before you take a break. All right?

A: Uh-huh.

Q: Any questions of the process, sir?

A: I don't have any questions.

Q: Are you taking any medication that would in any way interfere with your ability to give truthful and correct answers this morning?

A: No.

Q: Okay. Have you have sufficient food so that you're not feeling faint or have anything that would make you unable to answer correctly and truthfully?

A: Not that I know of.

Q: All right. So, you're prepared to answer my questions this morning, is that correct, Deacon Veereen?

A: That is right.

Q: Okay. For the record, please state your name and address.

A: George Veereen.

Q: And your address, please.

A: 1523 Cameron Court, Apartment A.

Q: Is that in Wilmington?

A: That's Wilmington.

Q: All right. And, you are a member of the Mount Calvary Missionary Baptist Church?

A: Yes, I am.

Q: And, how long have you been a member?

A: Well, I can't tell you in years.

Q: Well, do your best.

A: Since back in the 50's.

Q: Since the 50's.

A: Right.

Q: And, how long have you been a deacon?

A: Since back in the 70's.

Q: What is a deacon?

A: Huh?

Q: What is a deacon? In terms of this particular church.

A: A deacon is an officer within the church.

Q: You say he's an officer, and what are the duties of that officer?

A: The duties of that officer is to protect the church and assist in whatever capacity. Sunday school, Bible study or whatever.

Q: I don't really understand your answer, I'm sorry. You said your duty is to protect the church and then you said something about Sunday School.

A: Teaching and so forth and so on.

Q: All right. Do you actually teach Sunday School yourself?

A: Yes, I do.

Q: Okay. How long have you been doing that?

A: I've been doing that for quite a while. I don't do it constantly. We have others that come in and teach.

Q: Okay. But, approximately how long have you been doing that?

A: I'd say about—way back there. I started teaching Sunday School and so forth way back in years. When I first—

Q: So approximately in the 50's.

A: Somewhere about—I would say the 60's on that because I was in the military service when I first started.

Q: I take it then that you were a member of the Mount Calvary Baptist church, from now on I'll just use the word church instead of the long description, okay? Anytime I use the word church, you'll know I mean the Mount Calvary Missionary Baptist Church, because that's quite a mouthful, all right?

A: Okay.

Q: So, the church is the word we'll use. Were you a member of the church when the church approached Reverend Reddrick as a candidate for pastor of the church?

A: Yes, I was.

Q: Okay. And, would you describe the process of Reverend Reddrick being hired?

A: What did you say?

Q: What was the process that the church engaged in, in hiring Reverend Reddrick?

A: Because the pastor had died.

Q: Okay.

A: For their need for a pastor.

Q: I understand, but I mean what did you do in the process personally of hiring Reverend Reddrick? What do the deacons do, what do you do? If anything.

A: Normally in the church as it is, it gets a pulpit committee and the pulpit committee is one of that goes out and looks for the pastor.

Q: Okay. Were you on the pulpit committee?

A: I was on that particular one, yes.

Q: Okay. So, you're on the pulpit committee, and what actions did the pulpit committee take to seek a new pastor for the church?

A: They went out around and asked question and so forth.

Q: Do you advertise? Do you put the word out on—

A: The word was out there.

Q: Okay. When was Reverend Reddrick hired as pastor of the church?

A: If I'm not mistaken it was about '78 I believe it was. Somewhere in the neighborhood.

Q: Did you vote for him?

A: Yes, I did.

Q: Did the congregation as a whole have to vote, or just the pulpit committee?

A: The congregation had to vote.

Q: The congregation as a whole has to vote?

A: Yes.

Q: Okay. Do I take it as accurate then that absent the vote of the entire congregation in your church, Pastor Reddrick or any pastor for that matter could not be hired. Is that correct?

A: As long as the majority of the congregation say they want this man for a pastor.

Q: The majority.

A: The majority rules. That's what governs the church.

Q: Majority rules.

A: That's right.

Q: And, how did you inform the majority of the hiring of a pastor or the prospective hiring of Pastor Reddrick?

A: The majority is present at any particular meeting.

Q: Well, did you give notice of the meeting is what I'm asking. How do they know to be at the meeting to vote on—

A: You inform them.

Q: How do you inform them?

A: I make an announcement.

Q: From where?

A: You make the announcement from the church.

Q: From the pulpit of the church?

A: Not the pulpit. You don't make a—a deacon don't go to the pulpit to make an announcement.

Q: Okay. Who and how was the announcement made that there would be a vote to hire Reverend Reddrick? What was the procedure? Someone did something, someone said something to someone in some circumstance. Please describe that.

A: At that particular time, I was the chairman of the deacon board. I made the announcement that there would be a vote on Reverend Reddrick—Well, I didn't call him by name, but at the same time, it was voting for a pastor of the church.

Q: Okay. And, to whom did you make this announcement? To the congregation?

A: Made it to the congregation.

Q: At the Sunday service? Was it at a Sunday service?

A: Yes, it was at a Sunday service.

Q: I'm not trying to trick you, I'm just trying to find out what happened. Okay? This is at a Sunday service?

A: Yes, it was.

Q: And, did you do that one Sunday before the vote or two successive Sundays before the vote?

A: We did it one Sunday.

Q: One Sunday.

A: Didn't need to go for successive Sundays.

Q: And the majority vote rules today, okay. Now, what rules govern the operation of the church?

A: What rules?

Q: What rules?

A: What rules? Are there rules to govern the operation of the church?

A: Yeah. The church covenant.

(PLAINTIFF'S DEPOSITION EXHIBIT NUMBER 1 IS MARKED FOR THE RECORD)

BY MR. HUME:

Q: Are you familiar with this book? Exhibit Number 1.

A: (no response)

Q: Would you read for the record the title of the document?

A: Mount Calvary Missionary Baptist Church, 924 Northeast Street, Wilmington, North Carolina, 28401.

Q: And below the hands on the Bible, what does it say?

A: The Handbook for New Members.

Q: Okay. Do you recognize this document? Plaintiffs' Number 1?

A: Yeah.

Q: And, what is it?

A: All I know this is a handbook that he started since he come up—since he was a member of the church.

Q: He referring to Reverend Reddrick, the plaintiff in this case?

A: Right.

Q: Okay. And, isn't it true that this handbook has been given to every new member since Reverend Reddrick was the pastor and compiled the handbook?

A: Not in the beginning. This is something that come up during his administration. And that come up I would say five or six years before the end of his administration.

Q: the handbook came up five or six years, okay. And, from that time on was it not given to each new member who came into the church?

A: Yeah, far as I know.

Q: Okay. And you had no objection to it being given to the new members?

A: No, I didn't.

Q: Okay. And the purpose of the handbook is to, among other things, is to explain to the new parishioners the rules that govern the operation of the church, is that correct?

A: When you put the rules that govern the operation of the church, now, Mount Calvary Missionary Baptist Church always was ruled by the majority. We had no bylaws. We had no standard procedure in carrying out our business.

Q: You're claiming that the church has never had any bylaws.

A: Not since I've been there.

Q: Then, how do you function as a deacon? Under what rules do you function?

A: The Bible. B-i-b-l-e.

Q: Bible. Does the Bible have rules for organizations?

A: the Bible has rules—even has—

Q: Would you quote a section or two of the Bible which assists you in determining for instance a majority vote.

A: A majority vote?

Q: Yes.

A: The Bible doesn't deal in that.

Q: Doesn't deal in that. Is there anything in the Bible that tells you about giving notice of meetings?

A: It doesn't deal in that area either.

Q: Isn't it a fact, Mr. Veereen, that there's nothing in the Bible whatsoever that would tell a church organization what procedures on a day-to-day basis they should follow?

A: The church is a economy within itself. It makes its own procedure as it goes.

Q: Well, Mr. Veereen, if it makes its own procedures as it goes, are you telling me, sir, that every single action of the church is put to a majority vote?

A: Mostly. Any serious—any serious thing that takes place in the church comes through a vote of the church.

Q: Define serious, please. What do you mean by serious?

A: Things that when we go—when we go to our business meeting and we then try to pass some rule that we want to put into operation of the church—

Q: There are rules.

A: I say when we want to put something into a rule into the operation of the church—

Q: Well, are there rules—

A: Such as, on Sunday morning we're going to have church service. We're going to begin at a certain time, we're going to have preaching at a certain time, Sunday school at a certain time, prayer meeting on Wednesday nights and this kind of thing.

Q: So, there are indeed rules that were voted on by the majority of the church.

A: It's rules all right, but—

Q: And, where are those rules written down, if anywhere?

A: It isn't written down except anything—except in the minutes of the church.

Q: Rules written down in the minutes of the church.

A: That's right.

Q: Who decides, Mr. Veereen, what event is serious enough to put it to a vote?

A: Who decides it?

Q: Yeah, who decides it?

A: Ever who is in charge. Maybe—most of the time the pastor puts the—because he's the moderator and he's the one who puts it through the church. When they don't have a pastor, then the deacons go and takes over.

Q: So the written minutes of the church, who's the person who has control over the written minutes of the church? Who is the custodian of those records.

A: Church clerk most of the time.

Q: And, what's the name of that person currently?

A: I can tell you the one that we have now.

Q: Well, who is the one more pertinently in the last, say, two years of the Reverend's pastor there.

A: At that particular time, if my recollection leads me right, was—what was her name? I'm trying to think of her name. Annie Pompey, if I'm not mistaken.

Q: Would you spell that for me, please, if you can?

A: Annie Pompey.

Q: I'm not getting the last name. Annie, if you would spell the last name, please.

A: P—I can't spell the name.

Q: Pompey?

A: Pompey.

Q: Pompey, like the town in Italy? Or like the—

> MR. STEPHENS: It's probably P-o-m-p-e-y, but I'm not certain.
>
> MR. HUME: Like the politician. We'll resolve that obviously, counselor, between us.

BY MR. HUME:

Q: So she's currently the custodian of those records? The minutes?

A: Huh?

Q: Is Annie Pompey currently the custodian of the written minutes of the church?

A: Yeah, but the minutes normally stay at the church.

Q: I understand, but someone's in charge of—

A: She's in charge of it.

Q: She's currently the one who's in charge of it?

A: While she was living, yes.

Q: Okay. Who is the one who's in charge now?

A: Rena Lennon.

Q: Who?

A: Rena Lennon.

Q: Could you spell her name for me, please? Rena, R-i-n-a or R-e-n-a, do you know?

A: All I can you—

Q: That's okay—

A: I'm not high educated, I don't spell right, I don't talk right, I don't make announcements right. So, I can give you the name, you spell it.

Q: Try to pronounce it very slowly for me, if you would.

A: Rena Lennon.

Q: Rena Lennon, okay.

OFF THE RECORD
BACK ON THE RECORD

BY MR. HUME:

Q: So, Rena Lennon is the custodian of records of the minutes of the church.

A: Uh-huh.

Q: And the minutes of the church are where the rules of the church are written down.

A: Uh-huh.

Q: So, there's no document that you have taken the most important rules from the minutes of the church and put them in a written form for the membership, is that correct?

A: No, not to my knowledge.

Q: Well, you would expect you to know, wouldn't you?

A: Not necessarily.

Q: Not necessarily?

A: No.

Q: All right. Would you hand that back to me? Plaintiff's 1 please.

A: (witness complies)

Q: Thank you. Now, knowing that this was handed to every new parishioner who came into the church in what you described in the last five or six years, have you read this? And, are you familiar with its content?

A: To be frankly honest with you, I have never read it. To tell you the honest truth, I've never read the book.

Q: Okay. Having not read it, when it was starting to be disseminated, given out to—we always like to use some fancy words, if you don't understand the word I'm using, you tell me. Okay? I'm not trying to trick you or sound fancy, but we, unfortunately, have a tendency to do things like that. If I use a word you don't understand, please tell me to give you a simpler, better word. Will you do that for me?

A: All right.

Q: I'm not trying to trick you, I just want to know what you know and be clear about that and not have any problems later on. Now, knowing that this was being given out to new members and not having read it yourself, did you ask any of the other deacons if they in fact have read it?

A: No, I've never questioned it.

Q: Was that because you trusted Reverend Reddrick to put sensible information in the—

A: He was the pastor. He was the pastor and so I trusted his judgment.

Q: All right. And, did you know that it said, for instance, when services were held. Were you aware of that?

A: Huh?

Q: Were you aware that the handbook for new members, among other things, told people when services are held? Were you aware of that?

A: Told them when services were held?

Q: Were held, yes.

A: No. Like I say, I didn't read it.

Q: Well, did you have any idea whatsoever, Mr. Veereen, what was contained in this, whether or not you actually read it?

A: No.

Q: Has any of the deacons you've served with since it was introduced—

A: I think so.

Q: —read it?

A: I think so.

Q: When you say you think so, you think they've read it.

A: That's my personal opinion.

Q: All right. Have you ever discussed the contents of this with anybody?

A: No, not that I know.

Q: Was it ever—let me ask—go ahead, I didn't mean to interrupt you. Go ahead, that's not my function here to interrupt you.

A: I think at one point in time Reverend Reddrick went through that and discussed it with the Board or something like that.

I think so, now, don't quote me being sure on that because I'm not.

Q: Okay. Among the deacons, did you serve on the Board as well as the deacons, or is the Board of Deacons the same thing? Am I confused, is it the same thing?

A: The Board of Deacons is the same thing.

Q: Is the Board.

A: Is the Board.

Q: So you can use the deacons and the Board interchangeably, is that correct?

A: Yes.

Q: They mean the same thing, I just wanted to make sure. Did you ever hear anyone say that they had a quarrel, they took issue, they thought there was something wrong with anything in this new handbook for new members in the last five or six years?

A: Not that I know of.

Q: And, isn't this exactly the kind of thing that the deacons would deal with? What kind of information flow is being given to the congregation under the name of the church. Because it does have the church's name on it, right?

A: Say what now?

Q: Isn't it the function of the deacons to make sure that whatever is passed out in writing to the congregation under the name of the church is in fact truly reflective of church policies and procedures?

A: It's the responsibility of the pastor when the pastor is there. When we have a pastor. It's the responsibility of the deacons when you're without a pastor. We are only—when we have a pastor, we are the assistant to the pastor.

Q: You're the assistant to the pastor, okay. And, if you thought the pastor had made an error in disseminating this handbook, what action would you have taken concerning that error?

A: We would probably call him in and talk to him about it.

Q: and that never happened, did it?

A: Not as I know of, no.

Q: Okay. What is the church covenant?

A: I haven't been able to explain the church covenant to anybody. I could show you better than I can try to explain it.

MR. STEPHENS: Can we use a copy of it?
MR. HUME: Yes, please.

OFF THE RECORD
BACK ON THE RECORD

(PLAINTIFF'S DEPOSITION EXHIBIT NUMBER 2 IS MARKED FOR THE RECORD.

BY MR. HUME:

Q: Mr. Veereen, my copy of Plaintiff's Exhibit Number 2 and are we in agreement that your copy is the same?
        BY MR. STEPHENS: Yes, we'll stipulate to that.

BY MR. HUME:

Q: The church covenant, I would characterize as the basic beliefs of your church, the basic guidelines of how members—really basic theological beliefs and basic expectations of how the church will be run and how you will treat each other. Is that fair statement to make?

A: That's a fair statement.

Q: All right. Now, in your mind as a deacon of the church, what is more important, the church covenant or the law of the State of North Carolina if they conflict?

A: this as far as I'm concerned.

Q: As far as you're concerned, the church covenant—

A: The church covenant.

Q: —as exemplified by Plaintiff's number 2 controls if there is in fact any conflict between North Carolina and the church covenant, is that correct? Is that correct?

A: I don't understand what you're saying.

Q: Okay. The church covenant, if it conflicted with North Carolina law, would be what controlled rather than North Carolina law.

A: Right.

Q: Correct.

A: As far as myself is concerned, yes.

Q: All right. Do you think there's any doubt in the minds of anybody else among the deacons on that point?

A: I can't speak for anybody else, I can only speak for me.

Q: Fair enough. Now, this, of course, other than using the word majority, does not itself describe when church services will be held, correct?

A: Wait a minute, go back over that now what you said.

Q: Okay. It's not intended—the church covenant is not intended in any way to discuss things of a procedural nature—do you know what I mean by procedural nature? How things are done in the church. When services are held, when votes will be taken, when deacons meet, what deacons do, all of those things. Is that correct?

A: That's right.

Q: It's just not intended to do that.

A: No.

Q: The written minutes, in your testimony, they're the rules dealing with the nitty gritty, day-to-day, non-theological issues that you deal with.

A: Yeah.

Q: Okay. In this—we'll get back to this in just a second and I'll come back to—is it your testimony that you did not know that in the Plaintiff's Exhibit Number 1, the Handbook for New Members, there was a section in here called bylaws? You were not aware of that?

A: Because we never had bylaws.

Q: No bylaws.

A: Until Reverend Reddrick came there.

Q: Well, are you saying that these bylaws were never voted on—

A: Never—was never passed.

Q: Who would be the people who would be obliged to vote on bylaws if there were to be bylaws?

A: The body.

Q: The body of the church?

A: The body of the church.

Q: Body of the church, okay. And, I'm going to ask you a question one more time because I don't know that I got an answer the last time. Who decides what issue is serious enough to put it to a vote to the body of the church? Who makes that decision?

A: I thought I'd answered that. When we have a pastor, the pastor is the one that makes those decisions.

Q: The pastor makes those decisions. When we have a pastor, the pastor is the one that makes those decisions.

Q: The pastor does.

A: the pastor makes those decisions. When we doesn't' have a pastor, the Board makes those decisions, the Deacon Board makes those decisions.

Q: All right. Now, so it's the pastor's duties to make decisions on votes that go to the membership, right?

A: Oh, yeah, that comes from the pastor.

Q: So, the deacons don't have the authority to call a vote of the membership, is that correct?

A: As long as we have a pastor, he is the one that calls its.

Q: As long as you have a pastor—

A: He is the one that calls it.

Q: And the deacons don't have authority to call a meeting for a majority vote, is that correct?

A: That's right.

Q: Okay. All right. Now, we're going to switch gears a little bit here. Is the Mount Calvary—is the church a member of the Middle District Missionary Baptist Association?

A: Yes, it is.

Q: Okay. And, as a member, what does that mean in terms of the rules and regulations of the Middle District Association? What does being a member mean?

A: It means it's affiliated with for specific reasons.

Q: What are those reasons?

A: Well, such as missionaries. Such as outreach ministries and so forth and so on. Support of churches and so forth.

Q: All right. And, can you be a member of an association without subscribing to its rules>

A: It's not—the Association have nothing to do with the rules of a body of a church.

Q: Let me ask it a little differently. Can people be in your church, can they be part of your church association, and if they are there, are they bound by the rules of your church?

A: Explain that again so I can understand it.

Q: When people join your church or are a part of your church for longstanding, are they expected to abide by the rules of your church?

A: By the rules of the church, yes.

Q: Okay. How does the membership of your church and the larger association differ in that regard in terms of the rules?

A: Because it is an economy within itself. It governs its own self. The Association does not come in and tell the church what to do.

Q: When you say the economy, the church is an economy unto itself, I must confess I don't know what you mean by that. Could you explain that to me?

A: Self governing.

Q: Self governing, okay. All right. So, the Association has no authority to in any way insist that you adhere to its rules, is that your statement?

A: That's right.

Q: Do you know its rules? Have you ever read those rules?

A: What now?

Q: Have you ever read the rules of the Middle District Missionary Baptist Association, otherwise known as I believe the Hiscox manual.

A: the Hiscox manual is only a guide to be used if the church or the Association so sees fit to use it. That's as far—that's as far as the Hiscox guide goes.

Q: So, the Hiscox—

A: that's exactly what it says. A guide if you want to use it.

Q: It's not binding—

A: It's not binding.

Q: —on your church.

A: It's not binding on the Association either.

Q: Okay. So, is it fair to say that having affiliated yourself with the Middle District Association, you do not adhere to the constitution of the Association?

A: Go back and explain that again.

Q: Okay. You've told me that although you are affiliated with the Middle District Association, you are not bound by the constitution of the Association.

A: No.

Q: Okay. So, it is fair to say in summation that you can associate with the Association, be in affiliation with it, but you feel free to ignore any instruction or rule it might have within its bylaws or constitution? Is that fair to say?

A: That's fair to say.

Q: Do you know Reverend Reddrick's wife?

A: Yes, I do.

Q: How long have you known her?

A: As long as I've been knowing him. Just about the same time we met him.

Q: That's understandable. How well do you know her?

A: Not that well. I know her very well as a member of the church and the first lady of the church.

Q: Okay. Have you ever, before the recent events which we're about to discuss in some detail, had a conversation with Reverend Reddrick's wife? Please state her name for the record, by the way. Please state her name. The Reverend's wife.

A: Go back and say that.

Q: Please state—if I ask you a question that you don't understand, if I speak too fast, then that's my fault and you tell me slow down, ask again. Okay?

A: That's right.

Q: What is the name of Reverend Reddrick's wife?

A: As far as I understand it, it's Lorene Reddrick.

Q: Lorene Reddrick.

A: As far as I understand.

Q: Did there come a time in December when you had a conversation with Lorene Reddrick, the pastor's wife, about an accusation or suspicion that she made to you?

A: Yes.

Q: Before that you had known her for approximately how many years?

A: I would say about 13 or 14 years.

Q: So Reverend Reddrick has been the pastor 13 or 14 years before he was fired, is that right?

A: Yeah.

Q: Please don't put you hand there, it's tough to hear you when you do that.

A: It's a bad habit.

Q: I have many bad habits, but can we avoid them today. So, let's try to do that together. In that 13 or 14 years, did you ever have a conversation with Mrs. Reddrick, the pastor's wife, about any intimately personal matters?

A: Just once as I know of.

Q: the time in question that we're about to discuss, correct? In December of 2001?

A: Right.

Q: Is it fair to say then that your—the sum total of your communication with Mrs. Reddrick in the first 13 or 14 years was limited to pleasantries and church matters?

A: Right.

Q: Okay. And, as I asked before, did there come a time in December of 2001 where Mrs. Reddrick came to you and said she was looking for some sort of conversation that she wished to be held in confidence?

A: Right.

Q: And, what did you—when she asked you to hold the contents of the conversation in confidence, what did that mean to you? What were you promising to do when you agreed to hold the conversation in confidence?

A: I promised that I would not go out and deliberately repeat that conversation with anybody.

Q: So, that meant that you would not deliberately repeat the conversation.

A: Yes.

Q: Okay. And, would you to the best of your ability some nine months later recreate for us as close as you can the content of the conversation that you had with Mrs. Reddrick.

A: what you're asking me now is to go back over what was—

Q: Let me start again. Let me start again. Anytime I'm not making myself clear, that's my fault and you tell me to ask the question again. Okay?

A: All right.

Q: Did there come a time in late December that you had a conversation with Mrs. Reddrick?

A: Uh-huh.

Q: You need to answer out loud. So, if it's yes rather than uh-huh. Can you say yes out loud?

A: Yes. Yes.

Q: Okay. Do you know the date of that conversation? Do you know the date of that—

A: The date?

Q: The date.

A: No, I don't know the date.

Q: Was it a few days before Christmas?

A: Yes, it was.

Q: All right. And, where did it take place?

A: In her car.

Q: Okay. And, how did you come to be in her car?

A: She came to my residence to pick me up.

Q: And, did she call you in advance so that you would know she was coming?

A: Yes, she did.

Q: And, when she called you on the telephone, what did she say on the phone?

A: She asked what was a good time that she could come and speak with me.

Q: Okay. And, what did you say in response?

A: I told her in response the next day.

Q: The next day, okay. What time of day was it, if you can remember: Morning, afternoon, evening? To the best of your memory.

A: I believe it was late morning, I believe.

Q: Okay.

A: If I'm not mistaken.

Q: Late a.m. Again, all I ask is your best recollection. This is not a memory quiz. You were in your car or her car?

A: Her car.

Q: Okay. Was anyone else present?

A: No one.

Q: Were you sitting in the front seat next to her?

A: Yes.

Q: Front passenger seat?

A: Front passenger seat.

Q: Was the radio on?

A: No.

Q: Was there any outside noise that would in any way interfere with your ability to understand her clearly?

A: I could understand her very clearly in some things and some things I didn't get perfectly because her voice didn't carry too well. But, at the same time, I think I understand what she were saying to me.

Q: Do you wear a hearing aid?

A: No, I don't. Don't have one. I need it, but I don't have it.

Q: Okay. When someone says something to you and you're not sure you heard it correctly, is it your habit to sort of hope you've got it right, or ask them again to make sure you've got it right?

A: Well, it varies. Sometimes I hope I have it right and, again, I'll ask you—if I think it's important enough, I'll ask you to repeat it again.

Q: Okay. To the best of your recollection, what did Mrs. Reddrick say to you in the car?

A: The first thing she asked me did I—was I aware of anything that took place and I told her, no.

Q: Of anything that took place?

A: Yeah.

Q: How would that mean anything to you? That question.

A: It didn't mean anything to me because I didn't know where she was coming from. I didn't know what she was asking.

Q: Okay. How long did the entire conversation take place? How long were you in the car?

A: I would say maybe 15, 20 minutes.

Q: What was your response to the question, the puzzling question, were you aware of anything taking place.

A: What was my response to it?

Q: Yes. What did you say?

A: I just told her, no, I didn't know of anything that was taking place. Anything that was happening.

Q: Okay. What did she say then?

A: She said that she was having problems, you know, with her husband and she just wanted to know if I'd heard anything about it, and I told her no.

Q: Okay. At that time was it true that you were not aware that she was having some quote, unquote, problems with the pastor?

A: It is true, I did not know anything.

Q: You did not know, okay.

A: No, I knew nothing about nothing.

Q: At that time did you ask her what kind of problems are you having with the pastor?

A: Yeah.

Q: What did she say?

A: She went on to explain to me that she came home and caught him in a suspicious, you know, position with a young lady.

Q: Suspicious position with a young lady. Did you ask her who the young lady was? Or, did she tell you who the young lady was?

A: Yeah, she told me.

Q: All right. Who did she say the young lady was?

A: She didn't call her by name, she just only said that it was her grandson's mother.

Q: So, she used the word suspicious position? Suspicious.

A: Yeah, at that particular time, that's exactly what was said.

Q: What does suspicious mean to you? What did you take that to mean in the English language?

A: I took it to mean that they probably was doing something or saying something or acting some way that—out of the ordinary for a person.

Q: All right. Out of the ordinary. Now, did you ask her what she saw that was quote, suspicious?

A: I didn't ask her any questions at that particular time. I just waited for her to go ahead on and tell me what it was all about.

Q: Okay. Did she volunteer circumstances that led her to say she had seen—that she felt this was a suspicious circumstance?

A: Right.

Q: what did she say to you? What did she describe?

A: Well, she told me, she said, on that particular day that she came home and she finds Reverend Reddrick, her husband, and this lady in the den. I'm almost quite sure she said in the den.

Q: In the den.

A: In the den.

Q: All right.

A: Now, she also went on to say that the grandson was in her room and she was concerned because she thought that the grandson might have gotten into her medication. Not being, you know, noticing or being paid attention to.

Q: Okay. And, what else did she say to you?

A: How did she put that now. She said that—I can't recall now just exactly how she put it, how she framed this situation. But, anyhow she went on and said that Reverend Reddrick, you know, sort of give her some sort of cold answer or something of that nature, you know. But, she didn't come right out and—I can't recall exactly how she said it. But, anyhow, she went on and explained to me how this come about. She said that Reverend Reddrick had a habit of calling her and asking her what time she was coming home. But during this particular day, her cell phone was off because for some reason, she didn't go into detail why the cell phone was off. But, anyhow, it had something to do with her work. And, when she got finished with what she was doing, she didn't turn the phone on, she just got in her car and she went home. And when she went home, this is what she walked into.

Q: So, her husband typically finding out when his wife would return home from work was in her mind suspicious?

A: I don't know about that, now, I'm only telling you what—

Q: Who—I'm sorry, I don't' mean to interrupt, and I should not do so. Please finish your answer.

A: She only told me the information concerning the, you know, that allowed me to understand why that, you know, that she had the opportunity to walk in on the situation that she walked in on, which was catching him, I don't know whether it was in an indecent manner or whatever. She did not say that. She didn't go into that kind of detail.

Q: Well, when she—is there something else you want to answer—

A: Go ahead.

Q: I don't have any answers, you're the one with the answers here. So, I don't want to interrupt you.

A: Go ahead.

Q: Is there something else that you wanted to add there?

A: No, I ain't got nothing else to add to that.

Q: all right. Is there anything else she told you in that conversation on the 21st that she felt was relevant to her state of mind, visa vie, what her husband was doing or not doing?

A: Her state of mind?

Q: Her state of mind.

A: She didn't mention anything about her state of mind.

Q: Did she describe anything other than finding her grandson's mother in the den with her husband?

A: (nods head)

Q: Nothing.

A: She didn't say anything except that, you know, that she was suspicious that something was going on. That's all.

Q: What did she suspect was going on?

A: I don't know, she didn't say.

Q: She didn't say what she suspected.

A: She didn't say, but she was suspicious that something was going on.

Q: Is there any other thing she told you that you can remember now?

A: Not that I can recall right now.

Q: Mr. Veereen, did you make any notes about this conversation?

A: No, I didn't make no note.

Q: Okay, no notes. All right. Did you have a subsequent conversation with Mrs. Reddrick?

A: A what?

Q: I'm sorry. At a later date did you have another conversation with Mrs. Reddrick about what we've just been discussing?

A: No.

Q: Never?

A: No.

Q: How many times have you discussed these events—I'm sorry, this conversation since the day it happened? Can you estimate for us who else you've discussed this with?

A: I don't think that I can tell you that I discussed it with anybody. Only thing that I can tell you from here now is that I did not mention this to a sole, nobody, until sometime in January when I overheard a conversation between two ladies and then I knew that this thing was out in the public.

Q: This thing? What is this thing, Mr. Veereen?

A: The conversation that I had with Sister Reddrick for whatever it was.

Q: Let me ask you something, Mr. Veereen. Having heard that a wife came home to find her husband and the mother of her grandchild in the den, is that a thing? Is that an event?

A: All I know is she said it was a suspicious situation to her at that particular time. Other words, for me I didn't care one way or the other because I didn't have anything to do with it. But she came to me in confidence, but she did not say that she see him in any bedroom or any bed or anything of that nature. She told me that she was suspicious of something going on. And this is the fact that she expressed to me.

Q: She didn't tell you that people were disrobed or disheveled or anything like that?

A: She didn't go into that kind of detail with me. But I could tell from the way she was talking that she had suspected him and her in some role.

Q: Well, did you suspect him of something based upon what she told you?

A: Huh?

Q: did you suspect Reverend Reddrick of some culpable activity, some activity for which he could be blamed, based upon what she told you?

A: I could only take it for what she said, face value of what she said. You know what I'm saying? That's all I could do, face value of what she said.

Q: At face value, do you think that there's anything suspicious about a man being in the den in his house with the mother of his grandson?

A: I had no qualms with that at all.

Q: My question is—

A: I'm only saying to you that I was quoting to what she said. She was suspicious. I did not say that I was suspicious.

Q: Were you suspicious hearing what she said?

A: No, I was not suspicious because I had no reason to be suspicious. I didn't see this lady and I couldn't tell you anything about it except what she tells me.

Q: Since you were not suspicious, did you inquire further as to why based on the facts that didn't make you suspicious she was suspicious?

A: I didn't inquire about anything.

Q: did you ever at any time investigate her quote, unquote, suspicions?

A: I did not investigate in anything.

Q: And, what did you hear the two ladies say in January that you overheard?

A: I overheard them say, one said to the other, did you hear about what was going on with the pastor of Mount Calvary. And the other lady said, no, but I heard some rumors. And she said, well, what did you hear. And she said, well, I heard that the wife walked on him with a lady in the bed. And I was pretty surprised, shocked, because I know she didn't say anything about being in the bed to me.

Q: Who were these two ladies?

A: I can't tell you that because I was on a public bus and I don't know those folks.

Q: You don't know them.

A: No, I don't know them. If there's a conversation like that going on about my pastor, I wasn't going to identify myself to them as to who I was.

Q: I asked you if you knew them.

A: No, I didn't know them.

Q: Did you recognize them?

A: No.

Q: Okay. So, you have no idea even if they're even members of the church.

A: Huh?

Q: You don't even know if they were members of the church.

A: No, I know they wasn't a member of Mount Calvary.

Q: You know that they weren't.

A: If they were, I would have known them.

Q: So you're sure they weren't members of Mount Calvary.

A: Do what?

Q: You are sure, based upon your lack of recognition of their faces, that they were not members of your church?

A: Were not members of Mount Calvary.

Q: Any fool can repeat a rumor, correct?

A: Huh?

Q: Any fool can repeat a rumor, right, Mr. Veereen?

A: I can't—

Q: Any fool can repeat a rumor.

A: Oh, yeah, I guess you've got a point there.

Q: Any fool can start a rumor, would you agree?

A: I reckon so.

Q: did you hold Pastor Reddrick responsible for the rumors spread and invented by fools?

A: I didn't hold him responsible for anything.

Q: Okay. Now, did there come a time when you informed the Board of Deacons that there were apparently a rumor of infidelity?

A: Uh-huh.

Q: When did you so inform the Board?

A: I can't remember the date and time, exact date when this come about. But I informed them that—I asked them first did they hear anything about the rumor that was going around. And they told me no. So then I went on and told them that, you know, Sister Reddrick had come to me and state that she was suspicious of Reverend Reddrick about, you know, and the young lady which was the mother of the granddaughter. And, now, then I told them that I was not going to mention it to you, but when I heard this conversation on the bus, then I know the thing was out in the street, that y'all should know about it because the church's reputation is going to be at stake here if this thing continued to go on.

Q: What date was this meeting?

A: I don't know exactly what date.

Q: Approximately when?

A: Sometime in January.

Q: As a result of this discussion of people outside your parish spreading what you knew to be a lie, correct?

A: No, I didn't say that.

Q: Well, you did know that certainly there was no basis for what Mrs. Reddrick said to you to accuse the pastor of adultery.

A: To me—to me, I only know what she said, that's all. I did not take it upon myself one way or another. But she made it clear to me that this thing was supposed to be confidential. I was not supposed to get out and talk about it. And I didn't get out and talk about it until after that conversation I overheard. And I only talked about it then to the Deacon Board.

Q: Okay. Did anything occur as a result of that meeting with the deacons?

A: Huh?

Q: Did any action take place as a result of that meeting with the deacons?

A: Not at that particular time, no.

Q: All right. And this was in early January would you say?

A: Yeah, it was in January. Because I was hoping after the situation come about that Reverend Reddrick would have called us in and, you know, and said something to us, you know, concerning the situation. I mean, if Sister Reddrick suspected him of something like that, she must be confronted him. I was saying to myself why Reverend Reddrick wouldn't come and call us in and talk to us concerning if the thing was, you, was true and getting out into the street this way.

Q: Mr. Veereen, you've just said to me under oath that Mrs.

Reddrick must have confronted Pastor Veereen (sic) with her suspicion.

A: With her suspicion, yeah.

Q: Do you have any proof of that whatsoever?

A: No, I have no proof of that. I'm only making a statement here to clarify—to clarify my position and my frustration at what I felt at that particular time.

Q: Well, your position and your frustration was based upon a non-existent fact. Namely that Mrs. Reddrick had confronted the pastor with her suspicion.

A: I did not say she did. I said I was saying to myself she must have done it. This is me saying this within myself that she must have done it.

Q: So, you're holding it against Pastor Reddrick because he hasn't come to you to talk to you about something that as far as you know he had no knowledge of. Isn't that correct, sir?

A: Listen to what I am trying to say.

Q: I need an answer to my question, sir. You held it against Pastor Veereen—Pastor Reddrick, Mr. Veereen, that he didn't come to you to talk to you about something that you had no knowledge that he didn't even know about it. Isn't that correct?

A: I don't know.

Q: We're going to take this point by point, sir, I'm going to get a clear answer from you on this. You've testified under oath that you have no basis in fact to believe that Mrs. Reddrick did confront Pastor Reddrick about her suspicion, correct?

A: I don't have—

Q: You had no such knowledge. No such knowledge.

MR. STEPHENS:	Let him answer.
MR. HUME:	All right. Fair enough.
MR. STEPHENS:	Go ahead and answer.
THE WITNESS:	I didn't have no knowledge as to whether she confronted him or didn't confront him.

BY MR. HUME:

Q: You guessed that he had done so, correct?

A: I said I was wondering if she had confronted him why he hadn't called us in as a Board, as a pastor and the Deacon Board, to talk to us to see what we can help him do about keeping the thing under cover—solving the situation.

Q: While you're blaming Pastor Reddrick—

A: I wasn't blaming anybody.

Q: —for not—you said you felt frustrated, you had a position, visa vie, the pastor, because he hadn't come to you. But you've also said that you had no knowledge that he even knew what it was that gave you this position and caused you this frustration. Isn't that correct, sir?

A: I didn't understand what you—

Q: That's fine, I'll simplify my question.

A: You're going to have come a little better than that.

Q: I'll try to do that. I'll try to do that. Did you at any time ever ask the pastor, do you know that your wife has expressed to me suspicions about your fidelity?

A: Now, I was—

Q: Did you do that?

A: Understand what I'm saying now. I was not supposed to repeat this to anybody. And the only reason I repeated to the Board is because I find out through the conversation that it was already public knowledge, it was out in the public.

Q: Did you ask—

A: Now—

Q: —the pastor—let me ask the question.

A: Now, listen to what I'm saying. Listen to what I'm saying. I was not going to go to the pastor about something concerning his wife and his home. But I feel like if the wife had confronted him and whether this thing was true or not, I feel like he had the responsibility to lift up and say, wait a minute, this thing is going to get bad here, I better get with my Board and see what can be done about this situation. And so, I was hoping that he would come to us and say this.

Q: How could he come to you if he—

A: I would like to know how would I know whether he had any knowledge of it or not.

Q: Exactly, sir.

A: That's exactly what I'm saying. I was not supposed to talk about it, so therefore, I was not supposed to go to him and interfere in his private business.

Q: You couldn't tell Reverend Reddrick that his wife suspected him of infidelity?

A: I was not supposed to tell anybody.

Q: But you told the Board.

A: I told the Board after I found out that it was public knowledge.

Q: If you could tell the Board, why couldn't you tell Reverend Reddrick?

A: When I got the opportunity to tell Reverend Reddrick, we did tell him.

Q: When?

A: When he called—called a meeting and we come to the Board. He didn't call us t ogether, so we had to—so, we asked him about it.

Q: Mr. Veereen, you keep saying he didn't call you together. Has it occurred to you, sir, he had no knowledge that would be the basis for him calling you together? Has that occurred to you?

A: I'm only saying now that this was his wife. Now, I do believe if his wife come and got suspicious of him of something that his wife might have confronted him.

Q: Might have.

A: that's what I'm saying.

Q: Or might not have. One or the other.

A: That's what I'm saying, might have.

Q: Now, did there come a time—

A: I didn't know whether she did it or not.

(PLAINTIFF'S DEPOSITION EXHIBIT
NUMBER 3 IS MARKED FOR THE RECORD.

MR. HUME:	Forgive the endless writing on it. It's the only one I have, counsel. If you have a better one, I'd be very happy to use that one. It's the January 8th letter.
MR. STEPHENS:	January 13th.
MR. HUME:	13th, I'm sorry.

BY MR. HUME

Q: This says, and I quote, Sunday January 13th 2000, the board of Deacons and Trustees met with the Chairman of Deacons, that would be you, correct, sir?

A: Right.

Q: On Sunday, January 13th 2002 at 11:00 a.m. the purpose of the meeting was to ask Reverend to sit down from the pulpit with pay until the accusation against him has been resolved. And this is signed by John Green, Kenneth Drakeford, Rena Lennon and the Reverend Reddrick. And yourself., George Veereen. Correct, sir?

A: Right.

Q: Before this letter was drafted, what conversation had you had with Pastor Reddrick concerning the quote, unquote, accusation?

A: Well, we had our meeting and we asked the pastor concerning it. And he told us that he was not going to be interested in discussing any of this with us because he—it was his personal family and business and so forth and as far as he was concerned it was private and we had nothing to do with it. According to his—I'm not quoting him verbatim, now. I don't remember it verbatim as to the words that he spoke. But I do know this, he made us feel as if he would do anything and everything regardless of what it was to clear his name including sue and spend every dime that he has. Now, I do know he spoke those words. Those words he spoke. And he made us feel like, well, the church was not important to him at all, the congregation. Only thing that was important to him now was his reputation, regardless.

Q: Who wrote this letter, Mr. Veereen?

A: I don't know exactly who wrote this letter.

Q: You signed it.

A: But I signed it, yeah.

Q: What accusation in fact had been made against Reverend Reddrick?

A: Huh?

Q: What accusation had in fact been made against Reverend Reddrick?

A: We were only confronting him concerning the rumor that was out. That's all that this was. The rumor that was out. We did not bring any accusation against him whatsoever. Then, now—in the past or in the future. We did not bring any accusation or accuse him of anything.

Q: Until the accusation against him has been resolved. Those are the words of the letter.

A: Yes, I know.

Q: What accusation had been made against him?

A: that's what I'm talking about.

Q: What accusation—

A: The rumor. That's all it was.

Q: So you're saying that he was suspended because someone was rumor mongering?

A: That's exactly what's being said here. We do know that this rumor was out against him.

Q: Stop there, please. How do you stop a rumor, Mr. Veereen?

A: You can answer that better than I can. I don't know how to stop a rumor.

Q: You're under oath.

A: I don't know how to stop a rumor.

Q: Then how would Pastor Veereen stop a rumor? Reddrick, I'm sorry, I keep dong that. How in God's name—

A: We did not ask him—

Q: In the name of the Almighty, how did he—

A: We did not ask him to stop it.

Q: What did you want him to do?

A: To sit down until it was cleared up.

Q: How do you clear up a rumor?

A: All I know is what we asked him to do, to step down until things—the public knowledge now be cleared up.

Q: but you say you don't know any way of doing that.

A: I said that I don't know of any way of doing.

Q: Well, did the Board have some sort of thing it wanted it to do?

A: I don't know that. I don't know that either because I didn't ask. But at the same time, we knowed (sic) that if this thing continue on, it damaged the church. That we had to take action in order to preserve the church reputation.

Q: So, if people tell lies about someone in the church, they're expendable. Their reputation is expendable, is that correct?

A: I didn't start it and I didn't put it out there. Nor did the church did, nor did the board did. We only was approaching it the best way we know how to try to stop it or try to do something about it.

Q: And, what did you do about it?

A: You see what it says right there? That's exactly—

Q: What did you do?

A: That's exactly what we asked him to do and that's exactly what took place.

Q: What did you ask him to do?

A: Step down until it could be cleared up.

Q: How could it be cleared up?

A: I don't know.

Q: Did anyone know?

A: I don't know. I can answer for me, I can't answer for nobody else.

Q: I'm asking you, you signed this letter, what did it mean to you? Until the accusation has been resolved. What accusation? The rumor of adultery?

A: That was out of concerning him.

Q: But you knew that rumor was based on no facts.

A: I did not know that.

Q: You know the facts as known—

A: I did not know that.

Q: the facts as known to you.

       MR. STEPHENS: That's a different question.
       MR. HUME: Fine. You're right.

BY MR. HUME:

Q: the facts as known to you did not support an accusation of infidelity, did they?

A: Do what?

Q: The facts related to you, words related to you by Mrs. Reddrick did not support an accusation of adultery?

A: It didn't so far as I am concerned it didn't. but it must be for somebody else because it got out, right? And I didn't put it out there.

Q: I'm going to ask you this question again, Mr. Veereen. Are you saying that any time there's a rumor, it's the obligation of the person who's the object of the rumor to make it go away? Or, you make him go away by firing him. Is that correct?

A: That was not—that was not what I'm saying. That is not what we said or intend to be.

Q: What did you intend Reverend—

A: Only thing that we asked him to do was to stop down until this thing could be resolved.

Q: How would it be resolved?

A: All right.

Q: How would it be resolved?

A: It would be dissolved one of two ways. He could either sit down with him with all the rest of the people that it concerned and do something—figure out some way to do it. Which he refused to do. So, that left nothing to do but to take action that we thought was appropriate for the benefit of the church. Now, I'm only saying to you, what you read here actually took place. What you read here actually took place. How it was going to be dissolved or solved, I did not know.

Q: What specifically did you expect Reverend Reddrick to do from that point on?

A: Sit down and talk with us and see what could be done in order to do something about the situation.

Q: And, when did you ask him—did you set a meeting to do that? To sit down and talk about how this could be resolved.

A: Before this come about.

Q: No, after this.

A: Huh?

Q: Yeah, after January 13th.

A: Yeah, after that we asked him to meet with us and talk with us. Asked him to meet with the Mother's Board, asked him to meet with the Board at his house and talk with his wife. He told me I could come—we could come to his house and pray for his wife, but that he—he's sitting right there and he knows these is his words. That we could come to his house and pray for his wife, but as far as he was concerned, he wouldn't even have to be there. We wanted to sit down and talk with them, both of them at the same time. We have even asked him to bring his wife and sit down and talk with us and he refused.

Q: Did you ever speak to Nakita Brown?

A: What?

Q: Nakita Brown.

A: I had nothing to do with her.

Q: Do you know who she is?

A: No, never met her.

Q: She's the person involved in this rumor. You did not even know the name of the person who was involved in the rumor?

A: Do what?

Q: The person who was involved in the rumor. The mother of the grandson in the den on this suspicious occasion was called Nakita Brown

A: All right.

Q: That's the first time you're hearing the name Nakita Brown?

A: No, I heard it before.

Q: Okay. Did you or any other member of the church speak to her?

A: No. It was not our place and not our business to go and speak to her.

Q: Well, I thought you wanted to resolve whether or not the quote, unquote, accusation was true.

A: When we get together with him and his wife and see what we could do, then if this other party happened to be brought in, yes. But he was the key. He was our pastor. He represent Mount Calvary. And if, and if, if this thing continued to go out, it was going to damage Mount Calvary.

Q: And, would it damage him, this rumor? Meaning Reverend Reddrick.

A: Do what?

Q: And if Reverend Reddrick got fired on the basis of an untrue rumor, would that be damaging?

A: if he do what?

Q: If he got fired on the basis of an untrue rumor.

A: Look, I—

Q: Yes or no.

A: Listen to what I'm saying.

Q: I must ask you to answer my question yes or no.

A: I'm going to answer your question. Please let me answer your question in my way. If Reverend Reddrick had sit down with us and talked with us and tried to resolve this thing with us, he would probably be the pastor of Mount Calvary right now. But because Reverend Reddrick acted the way he did, that he did not care anything about the church or anybody else, then we had to do what he knowed that we had to do concerning protecting the church. Now, we give him the opportunity to come and help us protect him as well as the church, but he did not accept it.

Q: Please explain to me how him meeting with the Board could stop a rumor.

A: I'm not going to get into controversy answers with you on that because I'm no expert now, I'm no genius, I'm no nothing. I'[m only saying what I feel to be to be the gospel truth honestly before God.

Q: My question to you is how would a meeting with him stop a rumor.

MR. STEPHENS: Well, objection, he didn't say it would. He said it could possibly resolve the situation. He didn't say it would stop the rumor.

BY MR. HUME:

Q: You know that Reverend Reddrick—you know that you had no basis to believe that Reverend Reddrick had committed adultery.

A: I did not, I'm only going by what was told to me and that's all. Don't ask me I knowed this and I knowed that because I did not know.

Q: Nothing told to you—

A: I did not know that.

Q: —indicated that he had committed adultery. Correct? Nothing said to you indicated that he had committed adultery.

A: The rumor—

Q: I'm not asking you about the rumor, sir—

A: Listen to what I'm saying.

Q: I'm asking you—

MR. STEPHENS: Whoa, whoa. Let's just take our time. Are you asking him anything said

to him? And that could have been a
rumor or any conversation for about
six months.

MR. HUME: Fair enough. Fair enough. I'll withdraw
the question.

BY MR. HUME:

Q: Was there anything said to you from Mrs. Reddrick that
would indicate that in fact Reverend Reddrick had committed
adultery?

A: Not within myself to consider it. But I said this, she must be
considered it because she said it was suspicion to her. It wasn't
suspicion to me, but she said it was suspicion to her.

Q: Are there people who have unreasonable suspicions, Mr.
Veereen?

A: Huh?

Q: Are there people who have unreasonable suspicions?

A: I reckon so. But you're asking me for somebody else now and
I can't answer questions for somebody else, I can only answer
for myself.

OFF THE RECORD
BACK ON THE RECORD

BY MR. HUME:

Q: so, what conversation, if any, did you have with the pastor
between the January 13th letter and the day he was terminated
from the church?

A: We had about two or three different phone conversations.
The only other conversation we had face to face was with the
Board and him meeting and talked.

Q: What date was that?

A: I don't know exactly what date that happened. I'm not good
at keeping dates and all that sort of stuff.

Q: That's fine. There are minutes that will tell us that date, correct?

A: That's right, there should be.

Q: And, what date was Reverend Reddrick barred from preaching at the church?

A: That was, if I'm not mistaken, on the 13th. I'm not for sure.

Q: And, when was Reverend Reddrick terminated?

A: It was on the 17th.

Q: And, what happened between the 13th and the 17th?

A: Well, between the 13th and the 17th, we decided the fact that he wasn't going to sit and talk with us to resolve—to find any way of resolving the situation that we had to do something concerning the situation and protecting the reputation of the church. So, therefore, we decided to call the whole church in on that particular Sunday and ask them to set a time for a meeting to determine whether he would still be the pastor or not. And the reason for we asking is because of the representation of the church. So, therefore, when the meeting was called for that Thursday, we asked the church to vote as to whether he would be the pastor or nor.

Q: What date was that? That Thursday.

A: That was on the 17th.

Q: 17th. So, you said that the Board of Directors and Trustees met with the Chairman of Deacons on Sunday, January 13th at 11 a.m., correct?

A: Uh-huh.

Q: Were there any church services later than that on Sunday the 13th?

A: No.

Q: So that was it?

A; We didn't have a late service that Sunday.

Q: Right. So, how was the message given to people to come on the 17th?

A: Because we told at the church end.

Q: At the church end?

A: We held it in after the service.

Q: I'm sorry, when did the service end?

A: The service ended I reckon somewhere around about one.

Q: The service ended around one?

A: Somewhere around about one. Maybe—I can't be specific on that. At the end of the service, we held the church in.

Q: And you're saying at the end—1:00 o'clock approximately, whenever that service ended—

A: Yeah.

Q: The last moment people were in church worshiping God on Sunday, January 13th, somebody made an announcement that there would be a vote on the 17th?

A: No, we did not make an announcement there would be a vote on the 17th. We asked the church to decide on the date when we would meet.

Q: How was that decision made?

A: It was made from the floor of the church that we would do it on the 17th which was on a Thursday.

Q: so the people who were in church at or around 1:00 p.m. on the 13th voted on a date?

A: They did not vote at that.

Q: Well, when was the date?

A: The date set for the vote was on the 17th.

Q: Who set the vote? Who set the date?

A: If I remember correctly it was Chester Sinclair that made the motion for this date to be set. If I remember correctly.

Q: For a date to be set to do what?

A: To vote whether Reverend Reddrick could continue to be the pastor or be dismissed.

Q: For what reason?

A: For what reason?

Q: yeah.

A: What I just said. For protecting of the church reputation.

Q: What I'm trying to elicit from you, this is not a trick question, someone said something around 1:00 o'clock on the 13th to the assembled people in the church. And I'm asking you, what was said? To the best of your recollection, tell me what words were spoken to the congregation at that time.

A: We asked the church to set a date when they would come together and vote as to whether Reverend Reddrick would continue to be the pastor or be dismissed.

Q: Based on what?

A: Based on the church reputation.

Q: Is that what you're saying was said?

> MR. STEPHENS: Objection again. You need to ask him that, you didn't ask him that. You said—you're asking what the action was based on, not what they announced.

BY MR. HUME:

Q: What words were said? In case my other question about words wasn't clear to you, give me the words that were said to the best of your recollection. First of all, were you there at 1:00 o'clock when this announcement was made? Were you there? I don't want you to repeat what someone else told you was said. You were there.

A: I was there.

Q: Okay. What was said in terms of the meeting?

A: I just told you what was said.

Q: I'm afraid it's not clear to me.

A: We asked the church to set a date.

Q: Who? Who said what? Please tell me. Certain people say words, words don't come out of the air. Who said what and then someone else said something else. Please recite. Somebody said something and somebody else said something and then there was a vote or something. Please, I wasn't there please tell me what happened. Somebody said something about the meeting. Who said something about the meeting?

THE WITENSS: Where is he coming from now?

MR. STEPHENS: Who made the announcement to the
                 congregation.

THE WITNESS: I made the announcement to the
                 congregation.

BY MR. HUME:

Q: And, what did you say? What words did you speak to the
    congregation?

A: I spoke to the congregation and asked them to set a date as
    to when we could have a vote on whether Reverend Reddrick
    continued to be a pastor or be dismissed.

Q: anything else?

A: (no response)

Q: did you say anything else about why he would possibly be
    dismissed?

A: Yeah. To protect the reputation of the church.

Q: Are those the words you used?

A: That's exactly the words what words I used. To protect the
    reputation of the church.

Q: Okay. Now, what would that mean to people who didn't know
    of the suspicion that was voiced to you by Mrs. Reddrick?
    What would it mean to people, protect the reputation of the
    church?

A: I don't know what it means to them. I can speak for me, I can't
    speak for them.

Q: Well, Mr. Veereen, when you announce a vote to keep or throw
    out a pastor, did you think it was important that people know
    why they were voting?

A: Yeah, they knew.

Q: How did they know?

A: they knew that they was voting to protect the reputation of
    the church.

Q: The reputation of the church.

A: Yeah.

Q: Well, what was Reverend Reddrick accused of doing that damaged the reputation of the church, if anything?

A: We didn't accuse him of anything.

Q: Well, how would firing him protect the reputation of the church if you weren't accusing him of anything?

A: Because of the simple reason—for the simple reason he was the pastor. And this was public knowledge. This was public knowledge. He was the pastor. This was public knowledge. The members of the church knew this was public knowledge.

Q: How many people know of this vicious and untrue rumor?

A: I can't—now, you're asking and you're trying to ask me to speak for somebody else. I can't speak for nobody but myself.

Q: sir, you just testified this was quote, unquote, public knowledge. What does that phrase mean? Public knowledge.

A: Do what?

Q: what does the phrase public knowledge mean?

A: Means that the public know about what was being said or what was being done.

Q: did you not testify earlier that the two people you heard discuss this rumor were not members of your church?

A: That's right.

Q: Did you have any reason based on your personal knowledge or questioning of any people in your church that this scurrilous rumor had spread to your church?

A: Rephrase that to me again.

Q: Who, if anyone, told you who was a member of your church that they had heard this rumor?

A: If I can understand you properly and know what you're saying, I can't tell you or did not try to tell you that anyone told me that they know of the situation.

Q: Was there a single church member of your church who told you they had heard this rumor?

A: Only one that I know of.

Q: Who?

A: If I'm not mistaken it was only one.

Q: And, who was that?

A: I have to get this right because I don't' want to rock the boat here now.

Q: No hurry, take your time. You can take a break if you want. It's very important to me to hear this answer. If you want to take a break and think about it, that's fine. I'm breaking my rule, of course, but that's fine.

A: Did she say that? She directly say that—let me see how she put this thing. I don't' want to say exactly how did she put this, but anyway, she spoke and said that—no, seems to me like she asked me if this was—if this was true. And I told her I don't know for sure, only thing I know what was told tome.

Q: What was this, the quote, unquote, this was true.

A: Just a minute, I'm trying to get something in my head. Trying to remember.

Q: Why don't we take a break.

A: Because I'm a man that tried to be thorough with what I say. I don't think I'm going to even put this into record because I cannot be thoroughly sure how she phrased this thing. And I would rather not even put it into record—let it go into record that nobody not tell me to. I'll take that approach to it and I'll stand by that. I know it was mentioned, but I do not, cannot put it—cannot quote her directly and I'm not going to put it into—

Q: You understand I'm not asking you to be sure when you're not sure, and vice versa. You do know that, don't you? If you're not sure, I expect you to say so, or if you're uncertain—

A: I'm not sure and that's it.

Q: Okay, fine. Let's go through this a little more. Man or woman who spoke to you about this?

A: It was a woman.

Q: Parishioner or not?

A: Huh?

Q: I'm sorry. Church member or not?

A: Church member.

Q: Is it someone whose name you know but just can't remember now?

A: That's right.

Q: so, if you saw her at church you might recognize her and then you'd be able to tell me, I saw her face, I recognize this is the woman that spoke to me. Correct? That's possible. If that happened—there's a continuing obligation to provide information in lawsuits.

A: Yeah, all right. All right.

Q: Now, in some substance, I'm not asking you to quote her, in some substance, what rumor was she asking you to verify or deny?

A: the same thing that we are talking about now. The rumor concerning Reverend Reddrick and what was saying took place. I'm not going to jeopardize anybody but myself. I'm not going to say that she put this thing to me in a form, I don't know exactly.

Q: In some substance, did she go along with the rumor you had heard on the bus that accused Reverend Reddrick of infidelity?

A: She just asked me—let me see now. Seems that she asked me had I knowed about it or heard about it. I don't know. I'm not sure.

Q: Is rumor mongering a Christian thing to do?

A: Huh?

Q: Is rumor mongering a Christian thing to do?

A: (no response)

Q: Is rumor spreading a Christian thing to do?

A: It's not a Christian thing to do, but I reckon it's being done. Or, it was done.

Q: Mr. Veereen, when someone tells you they heard a rumor concerning infidelity, do you not think you have a moral obligation as a Christian to say, that rumor is false as far as I know.

A: I cannot say that anything is false unless I have the facts and know that It's false. I can't say it's true unless I have the facts and know that it's true.

Q: could you not have said to her, I know what was said to me and it didn't make me suspicious. Could you not have said that?

A: I could have said it in many different ways.

Q: Should you not have said that?

A: Could I have not?

Q: Shouldn't you have said that? Shouldn't you have said exactly that, as far as I know that rumor is false.

A: Yeah, I could have said that.

Q: Did you ask this woman how many other people she knew had knowledge of the rumor?

A: No, I did not question her one way or the other.

Q: And, so you have no idea how may people in the parish—I'm sorry, in the church, knew this.

A: No, I didn't have no idea how many really knew it.

Q: So, you say it could have been only one person in your church who had heard this rumor?

A: Huh?

Q: It could have been only one person in the church that had heard this rumor by 1:00 o'clock on Sunday, January 13th, 2002?

A: Anything is possible I reckon.

Q: Well, as far you know, there was only one. You have no knowledge of anyone beyond the one you spoke to.

A: the one that asked—mentioned something to me.

Q: So I ask you again, sir, when you made an announcement about the reputation of the church, what was that supposed to mean to people who heard it?

A: Again, I stated this was public knowledge—

Q: Did you mention in your statement about the meeting that what Reverend Reddrick had been accused of or what rumors were being spread about him?

A: Say that again.

Q: Did you mention what rumors were being spread about?

A: Did I mention what?

Q: What rumors were being spread about Reverend Reddrick.

A: In the meeting?

Q: Yeah, in church.

A: No, I did not.

Q: So you had no way of knowing whether this mention of reputation would mean anything to anybody who heard it other than this one lady. Isn't that correct?

A: Say that again.

Q: You had no way of knowing whether the mention of the church's reputation had any basis—had meant anything to anybody who heard it other than the one woman.

A: Well, all I know is that I asked them to vote as to protect the church representation and the vote came in.

Q: Well, let's go to the meeting now.

A: This is what I did and this is what took place.

Q: I'm sorry. How many services were there on Sunday?

A: Do what?

Q: How many services were there on Sunday?

A: There was one service.

Q: Okay. So, anyone who wasn't in church wouldn't have heard this announcement, would they?

A: Because it was announced again on Wednesday night on prayer meeting and Bible study.

Q: Okay. So it was announced on Wednesday night. Who announced it on Wednesday night?

A: I did.

Q: And, did you announce it in the same way?

A: In the same manner.

Q: And, between Sunday and Wednesday night, did anyone come up and say, what are you talking about, what's the reputation of the church—what are the facts, what are the suspicions, what are the accusations? Did anyone come up to you?

A: Nobody asked questions.

Q: Not a single person.

A: Not as I know of.

Q: Well, do you understand, Mr. Veereen, that there are an awful lot of people who are going to testify that they had no idea what they were voting on and why they were voting at the meeting on Thursday?

A: I heard that. I heard that.

Q: You heard that, haven't you?

A: I heard that.

Q: Now, don't you think it's incumbent upon you as the chairman of the Board of Deacons to make sure that when people vote they know why they're there and what they're voting on?

A: The reputation of the church.

Q: Well, that's kind of a vague concept, isn't it? Did you ever provide anyone with specifics between the 13th at 1:00 o'clock when you made your announcements and the vote on Thursday, the 17th?

A: Only one, I believe.

Q: I'm sorry?

A: Only one, I think.

Q: What was that?

A: That was—I believe that was Sister Holiday and she asked me, you know, concerning why this would come about and I told her that it would come about because the reputation of the pastor being damaged by rumors or whatever, whether it's true or false whatever, that we're asking them to vote to protect the reputation of the church.

Q: Did the church do or say anything in public or private to stop this rumor or tell people that there was no basis to believe the rumor?

A: Reverend Reddrick stopped anything the church could do by not cooperating.

Q: I'm asking you a question. If you don't understand it, please say so. Is there anything that the church did concerning the rumor to inform people that they had no reason to believe it was true.

A: Explain that now.

Q: did you have any reason to believe the rumor was true?

A: Me?

Q: You.

A: As far as myself, whether it was true or whether it was false, the reputation of the church was being damaged.

Q: So the truth is that is not important.

A: that is my stand and this is still my stand.

Q: The truth is not important here, just the reputation of the church.

A: that was my stand and still my stand. The reputation of the church was being damaged and that's what I asked them to vote on and that was it.

Q: And I'm going to ask you this questions again, sir, because you did not answer it before. Did the church do anything in an attempt to squelch this rumor, stop this rumor?

A: The church?

Q: Yeah, the church. Since the church was the one you say was being damaged by the rumor, what did the church do to stop it?

A: They voted.

Q: No, no, concerning the rumor. We know you fired the pastor.

A: Look, the church was concerned and they did exactly like I asked them, like I told them. The representation of the church was being damaged. You can vote to keep the pastor as pastor or let him go, because the pastor did not cooperate when we tried to get him to cooperated with us in order to protect him and the church representation. So, therefore, we did the next best thing, ask the people to vote to protect the representation of the church and that's what they did.

Q: What was said before the vote on Thursday and who said it?

A: I spoke and Deacon Canty spoke.

Q: Tell me what you said.

A: What did I say?

Q: Yes.

A: I told them exactly what—that this all over again, same thing all over again. We are here, we are not accusing Reverend Reddrick of nothing and we are not charging Reverend Reddrick with nothing. We are voting solely on the church—protecting the church representation.

Q: Who kept the tally of the vote?

A: What?

Q: Who kept the tally of the vote?

A: The tally of the vote?

Q: Who counted the vote?

A: Vice moderator Herron.

Q: How do you spell—Herring like the fish?

A: I reckon it's like a fish or whatever, I don't know. All I know is Herring. And Deacon Cox and Deacon Drakeford. Drakeford was the only member of the church.

Q: Was there any questions or comments from the congregation before the vote?

A: I think we had a few questions and whatever. I think we had a few question or whatever going back and forth, but it didn't amount to much.

Q: Didn't amount to much. What was the vote?

A: 60, 52.

Q: 60 to 52, okay. So, a few votes more than a majority. And by my count that's 112 votes, right?

A: Something in that neighborhood.

Q: How many people were in church on Sunday approximately?

A: Oh, I don't know, I guess pretty close to 150 or 200, I reckon.

Q: Was the church full on Sunday?

A: No, it wasn't full.

Q: Was it almost full?

A: Huh?

Q: Was it almost full?

A: I would say it was almost full. We didn't have that much vacancy. On Sunday church is always pretty well filled up.

Q: And, how many seats are there in the church?

A: I don't know.

Q: You don't know.

A: I don't know how may seats is in there.

Q: How were the votes made? How were the votes taken? On paper, hands, what?

A: Private vote.

Q: I don't know what that means.

A: It's like a secret ballot.

Q: Secret ballot.

A: That's right.

Q: And, what did the ballot say?

A: Yes or no.

Q: Yes or no to what?

A: to whether the pastor stay or go.

Q: What did Mr. Canty say before the vote?

A: I really couldn't tell you that because I didn't pay it that much attention.

Q: How long did he speak?

A: Just a few minutes.

Q: And you told the congregation that you didn't know whether or not the allegations were true.

A: I didn't get into that. I did not get into that at all.

Q;   You didn't—it wasn't important.

A: As far as myself was concerned, that was already solved.

Q: How so, sir? How was it solved?

A: When Reverend Reddrick refused to agree with us and sit down with us and—

Q: How would that have helped the church? Him sitting down with you, how would that help the church? How would that stop the rumor?

A: I am not getting back into that again. You asked me that how to stop. I'm no expert.

Q: You have just testified that the reason why you put this to a vote was that Reverend Reddrick wouldn't meet with you. You've also testified that the sole issue in your mind was the reputation of the church.

A: That's right.

Q: Putting those two allegations together, how would his meeting with you protect the reputation of the church?

A: if we all sit down and go and try to figure out how to do something, somebody would come up with an idea that might would work. But if everybody refused to sit down and talk about these things and really try to solve these things, nothing is going to work. And nothing did work because this is exactly what the condition that he put us in by not cooperating and giving us the opportunity to try to work out the situation.

Q: How did the Middle District Baptist Association come to witness the meeting on the 17th?

A: We called them.

Q: Who is we?

A: The Board meet and we agreed we would have, if the moderator couldn't come, have one of his representatives come and moderate this meeting.

Q: Now, when you say you need a majority vote, is that the majority of the members of the church of the majority—

A: Majority of the members present.

Q: Members present, okay. And, where is that rule written down?

A: that's a standard procedure in the church.

Q: Is that a way of saying it's not written down?

A: Do what?

Q: Is that a way of saying that it's not written down? Saying it's a standard procedure. Is it written down or not?

A: It's not.

Q: It's not.

A: but it's a standard procedure in the church.

Q: that's the way you've always done it?

A: That's the way it was always done ever since I've been there down through the years.

Q: So, is what you've been doing down the years, does that determine what's the fair way to do it and what's not the fair way to do it? Whether it's written or not.

A: As far as we as a party is concerned, we govern.

Q: You govern it.

A: We govern, not—

Q: Who's we?

A: The majority.

Q: The majority. Having called the Middle District Baptist Association to witness the meeting, they then wrote you a letter saying that they discovered that the meeting was null and void, is that correct?

A: Uh-huh.

Q: Is that correct?

A: Uh-huh.

Q: Are you saying yes: You have to answer out loud.

A: Yes.

Q: I know what you mean, but for the record we need to say yes or no.

(PLAINTIFF'S DEPOSITION EXHIBIT NUMBER 4 IS MARKED FOR THE RECORD)

BY MR. HUME:

Q: Now, why is it, Mr. Veereen, that having asked them to come witness the meeting and being told by them that the meeting was in violation of rules, you then felt free to disregard that?

A: That letter is stating that as far as they were concerned it violates their rules, not the rules of Mount Calvary Baptist Church.

Q: Did you think it was appropriate to give Reverend Reddrick notification of the meeting where he was going to be either fired or kept on?

A: Do what?

Q: Did you think that it was appropriate to notify Reverend
     Reddrick that there was going to be a vote on Thursday the
     17th of whether or not he would continue as pastor?

A: Reverend Reddrick knew it and we have a letter to prove because
     the lawyer written out the letter and tell us not to carry that
     vote through. So Reverend Reddrick knew about the meeting,
     so we did not have to send him a letter or a notice.

Q: Okay. When was Reverend Reddrick locked out of the
     church?

A: I believe that was—after the vote I believe it was. I'm not for
     sure.

Q: Did Reverend Reddrick preach on Sunday the 13th?

A: No.

Q: In fact he was not in church on Sunday the 13th.

A: He was, but he left.

Q: He left. Well, you told him to go away in fact, had you not?

A: Huh?

Q: He left. Well, you told him to go away in fact, had you not?

A: Huh?

Q: You told him to go away. He was stepping down until quote,
     unquote, this was resolved, right? Whatever that meant. So,
     he wasn't there when the announcement was made at 1:00
     o'clock of the meeting for Thursday, correct?

A: No, he wasn't there.

Q: Do you have any proof whatsoever that Reverend Reddrick
     was in fact notified of the vote on Thursday, January 17th?

A: We did not send him an official notice.

Q: Why not?

A: Because this lawyer wrote us and tell us not to go through
     with that, so therefore, we knew that he already knew about
     the meeting.

Q: The lawyer's letter says noting about a scheduled meeting, he
     just makes reference to your intention to vote on this issue.
     Isn't that correct?

A: Look at the letter and if the date 17th is not on it.

>   MR. HUME: We're going to mark this, too, unless
>   you've got a clean one. As usual, my
>   copy has a bunch of junk written on it.
>   Do you have a clean one? This is it, this
>   letter from my predecessor.

OFF THE RECORD
BACK ON THE RECORD

(PLAINTIFF'S DEPOSITION EXHIBIT NUMBER 5 IS MARKED BY THE RECORD)

BY MR. HUME:

Q: I show you Plaintiff's 5 which is a letter from Hall & Horne, L.L.P., my predecessor and attorneys in the action. Is that correct, sir? Is that correct? The letter from Hall & Horne, the attorney for Reverend Reddrick before I stepped into this case? The top of the page, sir.

A: Oh, okay.

Q: And, you are an addressee of this letter, sir? George Veereen, your name is here in the middle.

A: Yeah, okay.

Q: I turn your attention to the second paragraph, second sentence. We understand there is a meeting being called comma, exactly the nature of which we do not know comma, for Thursday of this week. And the letter goes on to ask you not to hold the meeting or if such a meeting is to be held that no adverse action is taken against Reverend Reddrick at that time. Did you upon receipt of this letter tell the law firm, well, it's a meeting—since they told you they didn't know what the meeting was, did you tell them or Reverend Reddrick, well, it's a meeting to decide whether or not to fire Reverend Reddrick?

A: I didn't understand what you said.

Q: When you received this letter, did you then notify Reverend Reddrick what was the purpose of the meeting on the 17th, Thursday?

A: No, I did not.

Q: You did not.

A: I did not.

Q: What are the rules that govern hiring and firing your pastor in the church?

A: Down through the years the rules of the church was if the pastor wants to quit and step down, he gives the church 90 days notice. If the church wants to get rid of the pastor, he's paid after for 90 days service. The pastor did not—would not have any obligation to the church after he give those 90 days notice. After the church pay him 90 days service, the church was no longer responsible for him or his employees any more.

Q: And, what about notice to the pastor that his termination is being considered? Are you saying there's no practice or procedure over the life of this church concerning that?

A: In our church, we don't need a reason or the procedure in order to dismiss the pastor.

Q: Is there a rule that says that someplace written down?

A: That's the procedure down through the years.

Q: You've just said that. My question is, is there a rule written down that way?

A: Now, there is some documents that state in some of the manuals of the Baptist churches the same thing that I just quoted to you.

Q: Do they also not say that the pastor is to be given—that the membership is to be given notice on succeeding Sundays of the coming vote to either keep or fire the pastor?

A: Not that—not that I know of down through the years I have never seen a note about that. That is Reverend Reddrick's written up things there. That does not stand with the party of the church. Those things are what he written up, just like the bylaws that he written up that were never passed.

OFF THE RECORD
BACK ON THE RECORD

BY MR. HUME:

Q: So then as I understand your testimony, for five or six years the new members were given without any complaint from the Board this handbook and this handbook says in pertinent part termination of the pastor at the term of office may be ended upon 90 days notice on the part of the pastor or of the church. Termination of the office shall be voted on at a special called meeting. Notice of such meeting and its purpose are to be read from the pulpit on two successive Sundays. The presence of at least three deacons and the majority of the members present and qualified to vote shall make valid determination of said office.

A: He written it up.

Q: And for five or six years, he having written it up, no one made a complaint about it or tried to prevent it's dissemination, that is the spread of this, the giving of this, to the people in the congregation, is that correct?

A: I don't know. I know I haven't.

Q: Do you know of a single instance where this handbook was criticized as contrary to the policies and beliefs of your church?

A: I did not know. Like I said, I have never read it. I couldn't tell you what's in there.

Q: I understand that you never read it. My question to you, however, is, during the five or six years this handbook was given out to all the members, was there ever any criticism from the Board or any members that the contents of this handbook contradicted the beliefs and practices of the church.

A: Not to my knowledge.

Q: Not to your knowledge. And you felt that you had no obligation to give the pastor any notification, either verbal or in writing, that a vote would be taken to keep him on or fire him on January 17th 2002?

A: Well, as far as myself is concerned, when I received the letter from the lawyer, that pushed it out of my mind that I should notify him. It was in my mind that I was going to notify him until I received that letter advising us not to have this meeting or hold this meeting on that date. So, therefore, I feel within myself that he have already knowed concerning the meeting, so it was not necessary for me to let him know of the notice.

Q: Mr. Vereen, when the letter says, quote, exactly the nature of which we do not know, referring to the meeting, how can you construe that language as giving him notice that there's a vote on Thursday to fire him or keep him on when the letter specifically says we don't know what the meeting is about?

A: Huh? He knew about the meeting.

Q: How do you know that, sir?

A: It's in the letter that there's a meeting that day.

Q: When someone tells you they don't know the purpose of the meeting, how does that tell you that they know the purpose of the meeting?

A: That he knows there will be a meeting.

Q: Yes, and he didn't know what the meeting was about. And did you ever inform him?

A: I did not say and I will not say that he knows what the meeting was all about, I don't know that. I said when I got it, I feel like he already know about the meeting, so I was not under obligation to notify him.

Q: Well, what's the relevance of knowing—

A: This is my personal self, now.

Q: What is the relevance of his knowing that there is a meeting if he doesn't know the purpose of the meeting?

A: I don't know. I can't answer that one.

Q: Has anyone kept a written record of the comments made before the vote on the 17th?

A: Huh?

Q: Did anyone keep a written record of the comments made before the vote taken on the 17th?

A: I don't know if we had any minutes written up on that or not.

Q: Who would know?

A: I don't believe any minutes were taken. I don't think any minutes were taken on that particular day.

Q: Now, you've testified repeatedly that you wanted Reverend Reddrick to come in and meet with you and his failure to do so promoted the vote to be set on Thursday. Is that correct?

A: That's what prompted me to ask for a meeting to vote, yes.

Q: Well, are you saying then, sir, that between 11:00 o'clock on Sunday and 1:00 o'clock on Sunday his failure to arrange a meeting with you is why he was voted out on Thursday?

A: I'm not saying that. I'm saying from the time that this thing got out and started, we tried our best, and Reverend Reddrick is sitting there, he knows that we tried our best to get him to meet with us with his wife, meet with the Board, about anything that we thought that he would submit to in order that we might work out something on the situation, and he refused.

Q: When did he refuse? What day of the week was that?

A: I don't know.

Q: Was it after the Sunday or before the Sunday? After the Sunday or before the Sunday?

A: Before—before that Sunday on the 13th.

Q: Yes.

A: He refused to meet. After that Sunday on the 13th when we tried to get him to meet, he still refused to meet.

Q: What was supposed to happen between the 13th and the 17th?

A: All I know is that anytime we tried to meet with Reverend Reddrick he didn't meet. He refused to meet.

Q: If a meeting between the 13th and the 17th was important to you, how come you voted for a meeting to fire him or keep him on on Sunday, the 13th.

A: We did not vote to fire him or keep him on.

Q: No, no, you set a meeting to do so on the 13th at 1:00 o'clock.

A: On the 13th I asked for a meeting to decide whether we would keep him or dismiss him.

Q: So there was nothing he could do between the 13th and the 17th, you already set a vote for his termination or not. Isn't that correct?

A: Do what?

Q: There was nothing he could have done between the 13th and 17th since on the 13th you had already set up a vote to determine whether or not he should be terminated.

A: Plenty could have been done if he would have met.

Q: Did you ever write him a letter saying we'll have a meeting to fire you if you don't meet with us between the 13th and the 17th?

A: Do what?

Q: Did you ever write him a letter saying to him if you don't meet with us between now and Thursday we'll have a vote to fire you?

A: No.

Q: Did you phone him and say if you don't meet with us—

A: No.

Q: Did anyone at the church hierarchy do that?

A: I don't know that.

Q: Well, do you think you'd know it if they did?

A: I didn't.

Q: Don't you think you'd know it if someone else had done it?

A: I couldn't say.

Q: If you find out if someone else had in fact written such a letter or had such a phone call, you will tell me, will you not?

A: If I know about it.

Q: Obviously if you find out about it, you know about it.

    MR. HUME: I have nothing further now.

OFF THE RECORD
BACK ON THE RECORD

CROSS EXAMINATION

BY MR. STEPHENS:

Q: The first question is just a matter of housecleaning, a real simple question. Deacon Veereen, I think when you began testifying you said that Reverend Reddrick was hired in 1978. Could that have been 1988?

A: Could have been.

Q: Because he had been pastor for 13 or 14 years.

A: Right, it could have been.

Q: Correct me if my recollection is wrong. I believe you had told Mr. Hume on his direct examination that the only person who had the authority to call a meeting of the congregation was the pastor, is that correct?

A: I think I did.

Q: Now, after thinking about that for a bit, is that a correct statement of the procedure of the church?

A: No, that was not really correct. Any member could request a meeting and come to the Board with it and if we have a pastor, then we could take it to the pastor and the pastor make the announcement. And if that procedure does not exist, the Deacon Board have the authority to call meetings.

Q: Is it fair to say it's typically the pastor's role to make the announcements—

A: Right.

Q: —and he would announce any meeting.
A: Right.

> MR. STEPHENS: I've got no further questions.
> MR. HUME: Nothing further. Thank you, Mr.
>   Veereen. You're free to go.

(WHEREUPON THE TAKING OF THE DEPOSITION WAS CONCLUDED)

GEORGE VEEREEN   02 CVD 0365

1   CERTIFICATION

2   I, Frances Y. Grice, a Notary Public in and for the

3 State of North Carolina, duly commissioned and authorized

4 to administer oaths and to take and certify Depositions, do

5 hereby certify that on August 15, 2002, GEORGE VEEREEN,

6 being by me duly sworn to tell the truth, thereupon

7 testified as above set forth and as found in the preceding

8 pages, his examination being recorded by me,

9 electronically, then reduced to typewritten form, that the

10 foregoing is a true and correct transcript of said

11 proceedings to the best of my ability and understanding,

12 that I am not related to any of the parties in this action;

13 that I am not interested in the outcome of this cause; and

14 that I am not of counsel.

15   IN WITNESS THEREOF, I have hereto set my hand and

16 affixed my notarial seal, this the _10th_ day of

17 September, 2002.

18

19

20 _Frances Y. Grice_

21 My Commission Expires: 04/10/2006

22

23

24

25

Page -101-

STATE OF NORTH CAROLINA   IN THE GENERAL COURT OF JUSTICE
                                DISTRICT COURT DIVISION
COUNTY OF NEW HANOVER   01 CVD 0365

REV. CHESTER H. REDDRICK,   )
)
              Plaintiff,   )
)
vs.   )
)
MOUNT CALVARY MISSIONARY   )
BAPTIST CHURCH,   )
)
              Defendant.   )
_____)

DEPOSITION OF JOSEPH CANTY

DATE: August 15, 2002

TIME: 2:30 p.m. o'clock

PLACE: Law Offices of H. Kenneth Stephens, II
           Wilmington, North Carolina

FRANCES Y. GRICE
Frances Y. Grice Court Reporting Services
Post Office Box 7064
Wilmington, North Carolina 28406
Telephone: (910) 686-4006

INDEX

APPEARANCES

For the Plaintiff: Robert J. Hume, III, Esquire
604-C Cedar Point Boulevard
Cedar Point, NC 28584

For the Defendant: H. Kenneth Stephens, II, Esquire
P.O. Box 2237
Wilmington, NC 28402

STIPULATIONS

It is hereby stipulated and agreed between the parties to this action, through their respective counsel of record:

1. The Deposition of JOSEPH CANTY shall be taken on August 15, 2002, beginning at 2:30 p.m. in the law offices of H. Kenneth Stephens, II, Wilmington, North Carolina.

2. Said Deposition shall be taken for the purpose of discovery or for use as evidence in the above entitled action, or for both purposes.

3. Any objections of any party hereto as to notice of taking of said Deposition or as to the time or place thereof, or as to the competency of the person before whom the same shall be taken are deemed to have been met.

4. Objections to questions and motions to strike answers need not be made during the taking of this Deposition but may be made for the first time during the progress of the trial of this case, or at any pretrial hearing held before any judge for the purpose of ruling thereon, or at any other hearing of said case at which said Deposition might be used, except that an objection as to the form of a question must be made at the time such question is asked or objection is waived as to the form of the questions.

5. Rules of the North Carolina Rules of Civil Procedure shall control the taking of said Deposition and the use thereof in court.

6. Except as waived by this stipulation, the provisions of the North Carolina Rules of Civil Procedure shall apply to the taking of said Deposition and as to their submission to the respective deponent, certification and filing, except that notice of filing is hereby given.

7. It is stipulated and agreed between the parties hereto that Frances Y. Grice shall be Commissioner for the purpose of taking this Deposition.

8. It is further stipulated that the signature of the witness to the Deposition is waived.

JOSEPH CANTY, being first duly sworn to tell the truth, the whole truth and nothing but the truth, on his oath, testified as follows:

DIRECT EXAMINATION

BY MR. HUME:

Q: for the record, please state your name and address.

A: My name is Joseph Canty, Senior. One Hampton Drive, Castle Hayne, North Carolina.

Q: Are you a member of the Mount Calvary Missionary Baptist Church?

A: I am.

Q: How long have you been such a member?

A: Over 50-some years.

Q: Over 50.

A: Over 50.

Q: 5-0.

A: 5-0, over 50.

Q: Good for you. Do you know why you're here today, sir?

A: I have a general idea.

Q: Do you understand that I'm the attorney for the plaintiff in this action—

A: I understand that.

Q: —Reverend Reddrick.

A: I've been notified by my attorney.

Q: And I will ask you questions now that you're under oath.

A: Uh-huh.

Q: And your obligation is to answer them to the best of your knowledge and to tell me if you're unsure of my question, if you can't hear it. If it's awkward, confusing, or whatever, please don't' answer it until you're certain you understand the question. Will you do that for me?

A: I will.

Q: Do you have any questions about what we're going to do today?

A: No, I don't.

Q: Great. Are you a deacon in the church?

A: I am.

Q: How long have you been a deacon?

A: Since '97.

Q: 19?

A: '97.

Q: 1997.

A: Right.

Q: Okay. Do you recognize the exhibit called Plaintiff's 1?

A: Uh-huh.

Q: And, can you identify Plaintiff's 1 for us?

A: It's a handbook for new members.

Q: As a deacon of the church, are you familiar with this handbook for new members?

A: I am.

Q: Have you read it?

A: Not completely. Most of it.

Q: Okay. And, may I ask you why you haven't read the whole handbook?

A: Well, I had a problem with it because of some things in there I didn't agree with. Such as the bylaws in there because I knew that the church never approved those bylaws and we have records to reflect that position that they never were approved.

Q: And, where are those records that prove that?

A: Where?

Q: Where are the records that prove the bylaws were not approved?

A: Where were they not approved?

Q: Yeah.

A: At Mount Calvary Church. In one meeting.

Q: Do you know the date of the meeting?

A: I don't have that exactly.

Q: Do you know the year?

A: Oh, it's been I would say approximately three or four years I would say. Somewhere in that time frame.

Q: Three to four years ago?

A: Right.

Q: Okay. And, if that's true, if these bylaws as reflected in the handbook are not accurate, why is it, sir, that you allowed new members for the years after you contend that these bylaws were set to be not approved to be disseminated, to be given, to new members?

A: As far as I can say, I had a problem with it and a lot of the other members had a problem with it. I never approved that handbook.

Q: Okay. And, what action did you take to remove these misleading bylaws from people who joined the church?

A: I mentioned to the Deacon Board that we should remove them.

Q: And, what was the vote of the Board?

A: Well, we never made a decision on it.

Q: Why is that, sir?

A: I don't have no reason why.

Q: Was there a vote to remove them?

A: There was no vote to remove them.

Q: No vote to remove.

A: Right.

Q: Even though you personally thought they were misleading.

A: Right, I did.

Q: Okay. Obviously other people didn't agree with you, isn't that correct?

A: Other people didn't agree with those bylaws.

Q: Well, some must have agreed with them or wouldn't there have been an unanimous vote?

A: Some of them did and some of them didn't.

Q: Who did and who didn't?

A: I couldn't answer that question either. I could answer for myself I didn't.

Q: Well, we know that. How many people were there on the Board at that time?

A: I would say approximately about five.

Q: Five Board members.

A: Five—let me backtrack that. You're talking about the whole Board, right?

Q: Yeah.

A: Deacon Board and the Trustee Board. I would say about five—I would say about eight people.

Q: Five deacons and three trustees?

A: Yah, I would say that.

Q: Okay. And, would trustees have an equal vote on this?

A: Sure they would.

Q: Up or down?

A: Sure. Before that was even brought to the church, the trustees and the Deacon Board should have reviewed that. Before it was approved, we should review it and approve it as a Board and then bring it to the church to be approved, which never was. Which it was, but the church did not approve it.

Q: they didn't disapprove either, did they?

A: yeah, they didn't—they didn't accept them, I'll put it that way. They didn't accept it.

Q: Well, if it was not accepted, why was it still disseminated as the bylaws of the church?

A: That I couldn't answer. Why it stayed in there, I don't know. I couldn't say that.

Q: Well, were you a deacon constantly from '97 until the present date?

A: Right. Right, I have been.

Q: And it's a mystery to you why the misleading bylaws were—

A: Right. It's still a mystery, right.

Q: Who agreed with the bylaws, do you remember?

A: I can't remember of anybody that agreed with them. Because they never were brought to us as a Board to be approved.

Q: And these are in the minutes of the meeting three to four years ago.

A: Right, they are.

Q: You wouldn't happen to have those with you, do you?

A: No, sir, I sure don't.

Q: Is there anything else in here that you don't agree with?

A: I've really looked through it and that's about the only thing—

Q: That's the only thing.

A: That's about the only thing.

Q: And, if these are not the bylaws of the church relevant to the issue of hiring and firing the pastor, and boards and committees, obligations of members, elections and officers, what are the bylaws?

A: The majority. The majority. The Baptist doctrine, the majority rules.

Q: Who has kept the record of these votes where the majority rules? Are they in the minutes?

A: Yes, sir, they are in the minutes. The church secretary has those minutes.

Q: And, what kind of things are voted on?

A: Well, anything. Or, if we're electing new officers, new deacons, new trustees, new presidents or anything of this nature. We carry a conference, it's a conference and the church votes on it.

Q: Who decides whether there's going to be a vote?

A: Who—

Q: Who decides whether there will be a vote? You can't have a majority without a vote, correct?

A: Uh-huh.

Q: Who decides whether there will be a vote?

A: Who decides whether there's going to be a vote? The people do.

Q: How do they do that?

A: They do it by making a motion from the floor.

Q: Motion from the floor.

A: Right, motion from the floor. They decide whether they want to vote on it or not.

Q: All right. And, other than people spontaneously making motions from the floor, is it your contention that there are not bylaws that run this church.

A: None.

Q: None at all.

A: None.

Q: Was there a conscious decision not to have bylaws at some point?

A: Well, I can't answer that question either. Since I've been there there were no decision to have bylaws.

Q: Was there a conscious decision not to have bylaws?

A: No. I can say no. Nobody ever brought it up to us. The only time those bylaws there were put in effect, not in effect, were brought up when we went to court to put two members, dismiss two members from Mount Calvary Missionary Baptist Church, Norman Lee Cromley, Walter Samuels and Mr. Talmadge, which is dead. And after we went to court, those bylaws was written up. After that incident.

Q: What did the court decision say about removing those members?

A: At that time they finally got a restraining order on them. They got a restraining order on them.

Q: Did the court say that there were in fact bylaws of the church?

A: No, no, no. Those bylaws wasn't—from my remembrance, those bylaws—

Q: Forget these bylaws.

A: Yeah, right.

Q: Did the church—did the court rule in that case that there were in fact bylaws?

A: No.

Q: They did not.

A: No. From my remembrance, no. From my remembrance, no.

Q: So everything is, you play it as it comes along, is that right?

A: Right.

Q: The majority can vote.

A: The majority rules.

Q: But there are procedures that determine when things get to a vote and how votes are made. Are you saying that every single thing that is voted on, to determine officers, determine deacons, every single thing is voted on by a majority of the people?

A: Yes, I would say the majority rules.

Q: How often does the Board of Trustees meet?

A: It depends, sir. When we have pastor, it was up to the pastor. He usually—he did mostly—he would decide when the trustees meet, when they needed to meet.

Q: How about the Board of Deacons, do they meet quarterly?

A: No, it's left up to the pastor. He met when he saw fit.

Q: So the majority didn't vote when there would be a meeting of the trustees or a meeting of the Board of Deacons?

A: No.

Q: Okay. That's something that was in the purview of the pastor, is that right?

A: That's more or less right, yes, I'd say.

Q: Do you know Reverend Reddrick's wife?

A: Yeah, sure. She was the first lady of the church one time.

Q: Okay. And, have you ever had a conversation with her concerning her personal life?

A: Never have.

Q: When did you first hear about—so, therefore, she never discussed the issues that are the subject of this lawsuit with you.

A: No.

Q: When did you first hear anything about the allegations or suspicions that she had concerning her husband's—

A: I can't remember the exact date.

Q: I understand that.

A: Okay. But, Deacon Veereen, he brought it to us one Sunday afternoon. Like I said, I can't remember the exact. He brought it to the Deacon Board, he said, I've been holding this back for a couple of weeks. And I've been holding it and y'all need to know about it. So, we asked him what was going on, what is he talking about. And he said, well, there is some rumors out about—I take it back. He said Mrs. Reddrick came to him and told him some things and he never accused him or never charge him of anything. He only stated that Mrs. Reddrick came and talked to him about some things that were going on in her house and that he needed to bring it to the Deacon Board and let us know, kind of be aware of what's going on. He didn't say what was happening or what was going on. That's the only thing he said. So, we got together, we said, well, we need to sit down and talk with the pastor about this. Because being Deacon Board, head of the church, that's our prerogative, we should be able to do this. So, we did, we asked Reverend Reddrick to come in one time, I think it was on a Tuesday.

Q: I have to interrupt you so the flow will work here. What was it that you were going to talk to Reverend Reddrick about?

A: What was it:

Q: Yeah.

A: About some rumors that—

Q: Rumors of what?

A: I don't know what they were because we never know—we didn't know what went on. We never charged him or accused him of anything.

Q: Well, you didn't even know what the rumors were about?

A: No, we didn't.

Q: Well, why didn't you ask?

A: Ask who?

Q: Ask Deacon Veereen.

A: He didn't know.

Q: He knew there were rumors but didn't know what the rumors were about?

A: No, he didn't. No, he didn't. But I don't think she really explained to him what the rumors was about or told him what was going on.

Q: You're asking—if you didn't know what the rumors were about and Reverend Reddrick—I'm sorry, Deacon Veereen didn't know what the rumors were about, what were you planning to say to Reverend Reddrick?

A: We were going to ask him what was going on.

Q: Well, if you didn't know—

A: What were the rumors out there about.

Q: Well, how was he supposed to know?

A: I don't know.

Q: How would you possibly respond to, so tell us, what are the rumors about you. Is that the question you asked him?

A: Well, after we got him to meet, that's what we asked him, what are these rumors, are they about, what were they.

Q: And he said I have no idea what you're talking about.

A: No, he didn't. What he said, he said, my wife spoke to two deacons. I didn't know which two deacons she had spoken to. And at that time, Deacon Nixon state, Deacon Nixon stated that I was the first deacon that she had spoken to. And we didn't even know that she had spoken to Deacon Nixon before she'd spoken to Deacon Veereen. We didn't even know that.

Q: Did Deacon Nixon favor you with some content of what she had said to him?

A: No, he didn't. He sure didn't.

Q: Did you ask him?

A: No, sir, I didn't.

Q: No one on the Board asked him what is it that she said to you?

A: Un-uh.

Q: Was that because it's not important what she said?

A: We didn't care what went on in his house or what she said. Only thing we were doing was looking at the interests of the church. That's the only thing we were doing. We could care—I could care less. I could care less what went on in his house. I would assume the rest of the deacons thought the same way.

Q: How did you know anything went on in his house if you didn't even know what the rumor was about?

A: Rephrase that again.

Q: How would you have any reason to think that anything went on in his house if you didn't know what the rumor was about?

A: Because rumors was out in the street.

Q: What were those rumors?

A: I don't know. I don't know. Members of the church or—I don't know.

Q: Are you telling me that there was never a time when anyone in your church said to you they'd heard a rumor and you asked what the contents were?

A: No, sir, I did not because I wasn't interested.

Q: Did there ever come a time when the Board discussed what the rumors were?

A: No, there really didn't. There really didn't.

Q: The Board never discussed what the rumors are?

A: No, they really didn't.

Q: You said they really didn't.

A: They didn't. I'll put it that way, they didn't.

Q: So, the rumor could be that the Reverend Reddrick was about to get to a toupee, would that be important?

A: To me it wouldn't. To some people it probably would.

Q: The rumor could have been about literally anything under the sun, correct?

A: Anything.

Q: And you had no idea what it was.

A: I had no idea what it was.

Q: But you thought that simply because there was a rumor, the content of which you know nothing about, it was incumbent upon Reverend Reddrick to come and explain to you something?

A: Uh-huh.

Q: How do you explain something if you don't know what the rumor is?

A: I'd leave it up to him. If he wanted to explain or—

Q: How could he explain what the rumor is if he didn't know what it was and you didn't tell him what it was.

A: I'll put it this way. We did not know what had happened in his house. Just like I said—

Q: Are you telling us that you didn't even know what the topic of the rumor was?

A: I want to go back. Yes.

Q: What was the topic of the rumor?

A: That she had caught some incidents going on in his house.

Q: Incidents of what?

A: That he was caught with a lady being in his house. That was the only thing that was mentioned, that a lady was in his house.

Q: Who was the lady?

A: I don't know. I have no idea.

Q: Would it matter to you whether the lady was a relative of his or not?

A: Like I said, it's immaterial to me, I don't care what went on in his house.

Q: You don't care whether he was guilty or innocent?

A: I don't care what went on in his house.

Q: I was asking you a question. You don't care whether he was guilty or innocent of this supposed event, is that correct or not?

A: Well, yeah, I care a lot.

Q: Well, if it's important whether he was guilty or innocent of some wrongdoing in his house, what investigation did you undertake to discover the guilt or innocence of Pastor Reddrick?

A: By having him come in and sit down and talk with us.

Q: Well, you told me before that you didn't know what the topic of the rumors were.

A: Uh-huh.

Q: Was that wrong?

A: No.

Q: Are you amending that testimony under oath?

A: Yes, sir, I will.

Q: You're amending that testimony.

A: Yes, sir, I will amend that.

Q: All right. So now you did know what the topic was.

A: Right.

Q: Okay. And, tell us what you know about the supposed incident he should answer for.

A: That's the only thing I know. That he was supposed to have been caught in there with a lady in his house. That's the only thing.

Q: Caught with a lady in his house.

A: Right, that's the only thing.

Q: What does caught with a lady in his house mean to you?

A: Well, he could have been caught in the house in a room, in the front room or living room. Just in the house with a lady.

Q: Well, is there something wrong with being in the same dwelling as another person of the opposite sex?

A: I assume not.

Q: You're a Baptist, not an Orthodox Jew or a Muslim, right?

A: Right.

Q: Okay. There's no prescription in your religion.

A: Uh-huh.

Q: There's no violation of God's law by two people of opposite sex being in the same house, correct? Or the same room.

A: That's true.

Q: Okay. So, what are we talking about here? Why would you spend five seconds on something that was not inherently, even if taken at face value, wrongdoing?

A: (no response)

Q: Or, was the implication that he had been guilty of infidelity with a woman?

A: I assume, yeah, I assume it's that. Yeah.

Q: So that's what we're talking about.

A: Yeah, right. I assume that.

Q: Why didn't you tell me that a half an hour ago, Mr. Canty?

A: Well, you kind of went about it around about way.

Q: Mr. Canty, my job is to ask you questions, your job is to answer those questions if you understand them.

A: Right.

Q: If you do not understand them, your obligation is to tell me that.

A: Uh-huh.

Q: I'm not here to play games with you, Mr. Canty, and you're under oath, you understand that?

A: I understand that. I understand that.

Q: Who first mentioned—

MR. STEPHENS: Can we go off the record just a second?

OFF THE RECORD
BACK ON THE RECORD

Q: What was the rumor?

A: The rumor was that he was caught in his house with a lady, a female lady.

Q: And you knew no other details whatsoever?

A: No, sir I don't.

Q: and you didn't care to discuss or discover any other details?

A: No, sir, I didn't.

Q: Why is that?

A: It didn't concern us really.

Q: Well, was the implication that he was committing adultery by being quote, caught with a woman?

A: Yes, sir, I would say that.

Q: And you're saying that the deacons of the board of your church, you didn't care whether the pastor was guilty of that or not?

A: Right. Like I said, it really didn't concern them. I mean, we didn't care.

Q: Then if it didn't concern you, then why did you want to talk to him about it?

A: Well, we wanted to protect the reputation of the church because some rumor—that rumor had gotten out.

Q: And, how did you know it had quote gotten out?

A: Because we've heard rumors from other people. From other people.

Q: Who specifically?

A: Well, I couldn't name them. Matter of fact, I even heard it out in the street.

Q: Tell me what you heard on the street.

A: Your pastor got caught in the house with some woman and so and so.

Q: someone said it to you.

A: Yeah, I just walked off from them. I don't want to hear it, don't bring it to me.

Q: Now, do you know that Deacon Veereen had a conversation with Mrs. Reddrick?

A: Yes, he did tell us that.

Q: And you know that Deacon Nixon had a conversation with Mrs. Reddrick?

A: Yeah, after we sat down and talked.

Q: And, did you ask them what she had said?

A: Well, I asked Deacon Veereen what she said and she said, yeah, he was caught in the house. She didn't say anything she caught anybody in the bed or anything. She thought something was wrong that the lady was in her house at that time of day. This was the only thing that he really said. That's what he said she said.

Q: Did Deacon Veereen tell you that he personally didn't find the facts as related to him suspicious in any way whatsoever?

A: No, he did not tell us that.

Q: Tell us what Deacon Nixon told you—

A: Deacon Nixon said—

Q: Relative to—I'm sorry for interrupting you. Relative to Deacon Nixon's conversation with Lorene Reddrick.

A: What she said, right?

Q: What he says she said.

A: Well, really only thing Deacon Nixon said that he was caught in the house with this lady. He didn't say what they were doing or anything. And he told her at that time that she needs to go and talk with Deacon Veereen since he's the Chairman of the Deacon Board. That was the only thing Deacon Nixon said.

Q: And, no other details were discussed?

A: No, sir.

Q: No other details were inquired of?

A: No, sir.

Q: No one asked Deacon Nixon, so, has she given you any rational basis for her suspicions?

A: No, sir.

Q: Did anyone ask Deacon Veereen if he felt that her suspicions were well founded?

A: No. Not that I know of.

Q: Wouldn't that be important to the Board to know whether or not this was the ravings of a lunatic or rational factual recitation of wrongdoing?

A: Uh-huh.

Q: Wouldn't it be important to distinguish those two polar opposites?

A: Sure, I would say.

Q: What did you do to distinguish those two polar opposites?

A: Well, we tried to get the pastor in and sit down and talk with him and find out things and see what really happened, you know, since the rumor was out there. Tried to get him to come in and sit down and talk with us and to work this thing out and see what really did happen.

Q: Did you talk to the person who started the commotion in the first place, Mrs. Reddrick?

A: No sir, we couldn't get to her. He would not let us get to her, because we tried two times. We asked him and her to come in and sit down and talk with us and try to work whatever problem there was, try to work it out. And he said no, if this had happened in your house—exact words, he said, if this had happened in your house, would you bring Mrs. Canty out here and have her to sit down and discuss that. I said, yes, I would.

Q: Do you know of any facts related by anyone that lead you to believe that Reverend Reddrick engaged in any wrongdoing?

A: Say that again now.

Q: Do you know of any facts related to you by anyone that would indicate that Reverend Reddrick was guilty of any wrongdoing?

A: No, I don't. I don't.

Q: Still today you don't?

A: I don't. And like I said, all the interest has been to protect the interests of the church.

Q: Well, what are the interests of the church? Is it an interest of the church to fire a blameless pastor because fools are spreading rumors?

A: I want to say something and maybe I'm not answering your question. But, we can fire your pastor any time a Baptist feels like it. He's a hired help. We can fire him any time we feel like it.

Q: My question to you was, is it in the interest of the church to fire a pastor who has done no wrongdoing but is the subject of lies and rumors?

A: If the majority of the church say so, yes, sir.

Q: Now, when you actually fire him, what rules determine the procedures for firing him?

A: The Baptist Doctrine, the majority rules.

Q: The majority rules—

A: Right, sir.

Q: Is there an obligation to give the person that you're voting on notice of the vote?

A: No, sir, it's not. It's the majority. I still refer back to the majority rules the Baptist church.

Q: Yes, I'm aware of that. No obligation to inform the pastor of the vote to remove him, is that correct?

A: That's correct.

Q: And, when this vote takes place, is the vote valid if the people who are voting don't know what they're voting on?

A: What are you referring to? You're saying that the people that voted that night did not know what happened?

Q: I'm asking you a question and I would appreciate your answering that.

A: All right.

Q: If the people who voted didn't know what they were voting on, would their vote be valid?

A: They had the opportunity to—

Q: Please answer my question, sir—

A: Yes, sir.

Q: —rather than the question you wish I'd asked you.

A: All right.

Q: Thank you. If the people who voted didn't know what they were voting on, would their vote be valid?

A: Yes, sir.

Q: Their vote would be valid?

A: Yes, sir.

Q: So they needn't know what they're voting on, is that correct?

A: Yes.

Q: Did you answer yes?

A: I said yes.

Q: Thank you, I didn't hear you. You have to answer out loud. It's just the way we do it here. I know it's annoying, but we have to do that. Are you aware of the fact that there are a substantial number of people who have in fact after the fact contended they did not know what they were voting on?

A: I'm aware of the fact of that. I'm aware of it.

Q: Does that trouble you?

A: No really because they knew what was going on.

Q: The question assumed and you agreed that it wasn't an assumption that it was a fact that there are people who have said after the fact they didn't know what they were voting on. You just agreed to that.

A: Yes, right.

Q: Does that trouble you that people voted to remove the pastor when they didn't even know what they were voting on?

A: In a sense I would say yes.

Q: But not enough to redo the vote.

A: No.

Q: Why is that, sir?

A: Because the majority rules.

Q: The majority rules even though they don't know what they were voting on?

A: Yes, sir.

Q: Did you make an effort to canvass the voters who voted yes to find out for sure if they knew what they were voting on?

A: Most of them I spoke with, sir, they said, yes, they knew what they were voting on.

Q: And, what was the margin of vote?

A: 50 to 60.

Q: 50 to 60, so do you know for a fact that there were ten people or 11 people who voted who didn't know what they were voting on?

A: No, I would say no.

Q: So, it could be that there were ten or 11 people who voted to remove the pastor without knowing what the reason was?

A: No, no.

Q: Well, did you take a poll or not? After the fact—

A: No, we didn't have to take a poll.

Q: So it's your impression—

A: Right.

Q: —that many people knew what they were voting on.

A: right, sir.

Q: There was no scientific poll.

A: Right. Right.

Q: Now, from whom did you first hear the allegations or the comments, I won't call them even allegations, the comments, relating to Reverend Reddrick?

A: the comments?

Q: Yes. The wrongdoing, the accusations, however you want to characterize it. When did you first hear that?

A: When I first heard it?

Q: First heard it.

A: I first heard it from the Deacon when he brought it to us.

Q: And that was in January?

A: Right, sir, I think it was in January. That was the first time.

Q: Okay. And he said the reason why he was bringing that to your attention was that he'd heard that there was a rumor outstanding?

A: Uh-huh.

Q: And that was more important than whether or not it was true.

A: Well, I would say in a sense, yes. Protection of the church, yes.

Q: Do you think the church had an obligation if they knew the rumor wasn't true to protect the pastor and his reputation?

A: No. I say no.

Q: No. No obligation?

A: No.

Q: Okay. And, just to be clear on this, you are stating under oath that you are sure that Reverend Veereen never told you that having heard what Mrs. Reddrick—

A: It's Deacon Veereen.

Q: I'm sorry.

MR. STEPHENS: Trying to elevate him.

MR. HUME: I don't know why I do that. It's a mental block in this case.

BY MR. HUME:

Q: I'll begin again. You are clear that it is a fact that Deacon Veereen never told you that having heard what Mrs. Reddrick had to say that he didn't find it at all suspicious?

A: I'm not following you.

Q: Did Deacon Veereen relate to you what Mrs. Reddrick told him?

A: Uh-huh.

Q: Did Deacon Veereen say to you that Mrs. Reddrick said to him that her husband had been quote caught in the house with a woman?

A: Yeah.

Q: Those were his words, caught in the house with a woman?

A: Yeah, those were the words.

Q: And, by the words caught in the house with a woman, you took that to mean committing infidelity?

A: No.

Q: You didn't?

A: No, I didn't.

Q: What did you take it to mean?

A: Well, I took it to—in a sense, yes. I'll put it this way, yes. I will say yes.

Q: So you did think that the way Deacon Veereen phrased those words to you that the implication was that the pastor was guilty of infidelity?

A: Uh-huh.

Q: Did you ask Deacon Veereen for any more detail:

A: No, I didn't.

Q: Did anyone else on the board ask for any more detail from Deacon Veereen?

A: I can't remember that.

Q: Did anyone ask Deacon Veereen in sum and substance when you say caught with a woman, should we, by that, mean that you're saying that Mrs. Reddrick is telling you that she saw her husband committing infidelity?

A: No.

Q: Well, did anyone inquire of Deacon Veereen just what it was he meant when he related these words to you?

A: I didn't. I don't know what the others did.

Q: Well, you were there, weren't you, Deacon?

A: I was there.

Q: And, did they or did they not?

A: they did not.

Q: So, a phrase is used, nobody asked any questions—

A: Uh-huh.

Q: —you think that he's been accused of infidelity through Deacon Veereen by his wife and no one asked Deacon Veereen to explain anything.

A: Uh-huh.

Q: At that meeting, did there ever come a time when anybody asked Deacon Veereen any further description or details of the content of his conversation with Mrs. Reddrick?

A: No.

Q: And you never spoke to Mrs. Reddrick on the telephone—

A: No. No.

Q: —or asked her to write you a letter?

A: No, sir, I didn't. No, sir, we didn't.

Q: And, did you at any time attempt to contact the woman that Reverend Reddrick was quote, unquote, caught with?

A: No, sir, we didn't.

Q: All right. What investigation did the Board conduct into this incident?

A: The only thing we really did, we asked Reverend Reddrick— maybe I'm not answering the question. We asked Reverend Reddrick could we have him and Mrs. Reddrick—could we come out and see Mrs. Reddrick and talk to her. And that was before we went downtown to the courthouse the last time. And it was said, Deacon Veereen called and he said, no, Reverend Reddrick refused to let him come over there to talk to her.

Q: Isn't it a fact, Deacon Canty, the call was made on a work day when you knew Mrs. Reddrick had to go to work?

A: That was 5:00 o'clock in the afternoon, sir.

Q: 5:00 o'clock in the afternoon.

A: Yes.

Q: So, if Reverend Reddrick testifies it was in the morning, he'd be incorrect?

A: Yes, sir. Because I knew Deacon Veereen—he called to make it that afternoon.

Q: How do you know that? Did you see it?

A: I heard, he called me and told me he did.

Q: You don't have any knowledge of your own that that happened.

A: No, I couldn't say, but I—

Q: It just was the Deacon told you.

A: Right. Right, sir. Yes, sir.

Q: Okay. All right, Deacon. Now, do you know Willie Lee Brown?

A: Yes, sir, I do.

Q: Is he a member of your congregation?

A: He was.

Q: Okay. Has he since left the church?

A: Far as I know he has. He hasn't been back since.

Q: Now, Willie Lee Brown—let me go back a second. Did there come a time that you visited Mr. Brown at his home?

A: Uh-huh.

Q: Okay. Was that the day before or the night before the vote to terminate—

A: No, it wasn't. It was a couple of days before that. I stopped by because I went by, he was supposed to purchase.

Q: He was going to look at a what:

A: A car.

Q: A car, okay.

A: That I was supposed to purchase. And we talked. We talked and he—like we normally do. Because we had a pretty good relationship. And at the time I brought up—I must be truthful and honest, I brought up the pastor. I said, there's some allegation out there about our pastor I don't like. People coming up to me talking and I don't want them talking to me about this. And this is all I really say to him. I didn't say anything to him about trying to have him to go or swing either way. I wasn't going against the pastor or with the pastor. That's what we talked about. I didn't stay there but about five or ten minutes with him.

Q: What was the car that you were looking at?

A: Some car next door at the lot next to where he lives at. And I asked him about it, I wanted to buy it for parts.

Q: Was it his car?

A: No, sir, it was another guy. He was supposed to ask this guy about selling me the car.

Q: Why was he involved in a car he didn't own—the sale of a car he didn't own?

A: I don't know why. I asked—I looked at the car prior and I asked him to ask the guy did he want to sell that car. And he said he would ask the guy if he wanted to sell the car. So, I said go ahead and ask him, so I stopped by to talk with him about the car. And at that time, like I said, I said—we started talking and I said Willie Lee, there's some allegations out there about our pastor I don't like and people coming up and talking about it and I don't appreciate it. That's the exact words I told him.

Q: Did the car had a for sale sign on it?

A: No, it did not. Did not.

Q: What prompted you then to ask him about the car? What did you think—

A: I asked him prior to all this came about.

Q: I understand that. I mean, on any given street there are 20, 30 cars parked. What would possibly prompt you to ask him about a car that he didn't own?

A: Because he knew the guy.

Q: How did you know that?

A: He told me.

Q: Well, why would he tell you?

A: Because I asked him to see the guy, to find out who owned the car. And he said he would, and he did. He went back and he found—I forget the guy's name, but he did go back and he found out the guy that owned the car.

Q: And having found that out, why did you not then deal directly with the owner of the car?

A: Because he did not tell me where the guy lived at. I went back by his house to find out where the guy lived at. That's the reason I went by his house.

Q: Did you tell Mr. Brown that Mrs. Reddrick told Deacon Veereen she caught Reverend Reddrick—

A: No, I did not.

Q: You have to let me finish. I'm sorry, it's just the way we do things.

MR. STEPHENS: Let him finish the question.

BY MR. HUME:

Q: What question did you think you were answering, sir? Why did you interrupt my question before I finished it? What were you denying, sir, when I hadn't finished my question?

A: No, I wasn't denying anything.

Q: Well, you were jumping up to deny something and I hadn't even finished the question.

A: I was listening at the question you was asking me. You sound like you was asking me did I tell Willie Lee that Mrs. Reddrick had said something or didn't really say something about Mr. Reddrick. That's why I say that.

Q: Is it your testimony here under oath that you did not tell Mr. Brown that Mrs. Reddrick had told Deacon Veereen that she'd caught Reverend Reddrick and a young woman having sex in the Reddrick home?

A: No. No, I did not say that.

Q: So, when Willie Lee Brown testifies under oath, he'd be incorrect when he says that, is that right?

A: Yes, sir.

Q: And, did Mr. Brown ask you about proof of the allegations?

A: No, he didn't. He didn't ask me anything like that, sir.

Q: And, did Mr. Brown tell you sir, that it was wrong for the deacons to try to convince church members to vote Reverend Reddrick out of the church without any proof of an allegation?

A: No, sir, he never did say that.

Q: He never said that.

A: No, sir.

Q: Any reason why he would make this up to contradict you?

A: I have no idea, sir.

Q: Does he have a grudge against you?

A: I don't want to answer that question, sir.

Q: Well, you must answer it.

A: I think he does.

Q: Why, sir:

A: I don't know. I have no idea, sir.

Q: And, when did this grudge begin, sir?

A: It's been going on quite a while.

Q: And, how does it manifest itself?

A: I don't know. This came up in Sunday school.

Q: How long ago?

A: Oh, I'll say at least about a year. Maybe a little longer than a year.

Q: Notwithstanding that fact, you're going over to his house to ask about a car next door.

A: yeah, I went there.

Q: You told Mr. Brown we don't want him there no more. Did you say that to Mr. Brown?

A: No, sir. No, sir.

Q: All right. Now, Mr. Brown also says he was at the meeting on the 17th. Do you know if that's true or not?

A: Yeah, he was there.

Q: Okay. He characterizes you as the main spokesman for the church, is that correct? Is that fair to say?

A: In what respect, sir?

Q: Well, did you speak the most at the meeting where Reverend Reddrick was voted out?

A: No, sir, the only—matter of fact, I recall when he was voted out, I didn't say anything, sir.

Q: So, when Deacon Veereen testified under oath that you indeed made extensive comments compared to his, he would be wrong?

A: I would say, yes. I really would say yes, sir.

Q: Now, what did—if you said nothing, I won't ask you what you said, obviously, what did Deacon Veereen say?

A: At which meeting? May I ask which meeting are you talking about, sir?

Q: Was there more than one meeting on January 17th?

A: When he was voted out?

Q: I think that's what my question was, wasn't it?

A: Right.

Q: Any confusion in that?

A: No, sir.

Q: Thank you. Let's go back. We're talking about the January 17th meeting where Reverend Reddrick was voted out.

A: Okay.

Q: We agree on that, right?

A: Uh-huh.

Q: We're solid on that.

A: Uh-huh.

Q: And you're saying that you said nothing.

A: No, I said I didn't.

Q: You said nothing.

A: I didn't say anything.

Q: Who did speak?

A: The moderator and the assistant that he had there with him.

Q: Who was the moderator, please?

A: Dr. Carr.

Q: Dr. Carr?

A: Right. From the Middle District Association.

Q: Yes, and what did he say. Just stop for a minute, please, what did he say?

A: He said we're here to vote tonight on whether the pastor—whether to retain the pastor or dismiss the pastor.

Q: And, why was he speaking?

A: Because he was running the meeting, sir.

Q: Say again.

A: He was running the meeting. He was conducting the meeting.

Q: Are you a member of the Baptist Convention that he represents?

A: The Association?

Q: Yes.

A: Yes, sir, we are.

Q: Okay. And, do you have to follow the rules of the Association?

A: No, sir, we don't.

Q: So, you're a member of it but you don't have to follow the rules of it.

A: don't have to follow it.

Q: What was he doing there then? If the rules of his association were not binding on the meeting, why, sir, is he there?

A: Can I answer this way. The Association, if we need help from the Association, they don't tell us what to do. They don't tell us what to do, they can't run our church. But if we need help, we're a member of that Association, if we need help, we can ask them to come in and help us.

Q: What help did you want?

A: We wanted them to come in and conduct that meeting.

Q: Why?

A; So we'll be legal, sir. So they'll be no conflict or anything. Somebody saying you're doing something wrong. That's why we asked them to come in and conduct it.

Q: In fact, having the been there, the Middle District told you that they felt misled, didn't they?

A: No, sir, they didn't. When Dr. Carr came in, and he did not—the night he conduct that meeting, he did not say that he felt misled. Matter of fact, he said everything was in order and he seen nothing wrong with it.

Q: Plaintiff's Number 4, let's see if we have a copy of that to give you, let's see if you've ever seen that.

MR. STEPHENS:	What was it?
MR. HUME:	This was the letter from the Middle District. I'll find one. I'll give him my messy copy.
MR. STEPHENS:	What's the date of it?
MR. HUME:	It's the January 24th.
MR. STEPHENS:	I've got one right here if you want one.
MR. HUME:	Yeah, if you would. I thought I had a messy copy.

MR. STEPHENS: Do you want to do another one?

MR. HUME: No, I'll just show it to him. I
                 don't want to take any more time
                 unnecessarily.

BY MR. HUME:

Q: I ask you if you recognize that, Plaintiff's Exhibit 4?

A: I've seen this letter yes, sir.

Q: Your counsel is going to show you a copy of this. The moderator
      and the executive board feel as though we were misinformed.
      Therefore, all action items in this particular meeting are
      considered null and void. Now, I asked you before if Mr.
      Carr didn't feel he was mislead. You said—you denied that.
      And yet the letter specifically says, we feel as though we were
      misinformed. Therefore, all actions at this particular meeting are
      considered null and void. Do you know what that means?

A: Yes, sir.

Q: And you ignored it, knowing what it meant.

A: I've read the letter.

Q: Right, you said that.

A: And, I need to comment on that, sir. Can I?

Q: Go ahead.

A: All right. That letter was written after the vote. After Moderator
      Carr did that meeting, that letter was written after that meeting
      was held. And that's why I said—it was written after that
      meeting was held on that 17th.

Q: Of course it was, it's dated January 24th.

A: Right. Right.

Q: We all agree on that.

A: All right. Dr. Carr, we have in the minutes where the clerk took
      the minutes that Dr. Carr said that the meeting was legitimate
      and he saw nothing that was taking place that was out of the
      ordinary.

Q: All right. The letter specifically says in paragraph three, since
      then the Board has been informed that all members were

not contacted and told specifically they would be voting on retaining or dismissing their pastor. And in the paragraph you see we understand that the pastor was not even aware of this meeting. In fact, both of those things are in fact correct. That not all members were contacted and not all members were specifically told that they would be voting on retaining or dismissing the pastor. Do you not agree that those are facts correctly stated by Reverend Carr in this letter from the Middle District Baptist Association.

A: Read the first one. You said—read the first one.

Q: Since then the Board has been informed that all members were not contacted and told specifically that they would be voting on retaining or dismissing their pastor.

A: Uh-huh.

Q: and then also he says, we understand that the pastor was not even aware of this meeting.

A: The pastor was aware of that meeting because Deacon Nixon told him. Deacon Nixon told him.

Q: When did Deacon Nixon—did Deacon Nixon do that in your presence?

A: No, sir, he didn't do it in my presence.

Q: He related to you—

A: He related to me that he did tell him.

Q: Did he tell him that the that the purpose—let me rephrase that. Did Deacon Nixon tell you that he told my client that the purpose of the meeting was to retain him or terminate him?

A: I'm assuming he did.

Q: So he didn't specifically tell you that he told him what the purpose of the meeting was.

A: No, sir.

Q: You're assuming.

A: Yes, sir. He did tell him there was a meeting though.

Q: We all agree that my client knew there was a meeting.

A: Uh-huh.

Q: But, we haven't heard any proof that he knew what was going on at the meeting. Now, do you have any other proof that my client knew what the purpose of the meeting was on January 17th?

A: I would have no idea, sir.

Q: And, what notification did the membership of the church get about the January 17th meeting?

A: That Sunday afternoon it was mentioned by Deacon Veereen. It was announced. The congregation held there. It was announced that Sunday afternoon. And Wednesday.

Q: That what?

A: the meeting would be held.

Q: To do what?

A: To determine whether we maintain the pastor or to keep the pastor.

Q: Okay. Did Reverend Carr know anything about whether or not you'd maintain the pastor or keep the pastor?

A: Yes, sir, he knew it. He knew that when Deacon Veereen—I'm assuming—I'll put it this way. Deacon Veereen informed him that what the purpose of the meeting was. He did.

Q: I would ask you, I know this is tough, please don't assume. It's just going to waste time.

A: Okay.

Q: Fair enough.

A: Fair enough.

Q: To your knowledge did Reverend Carr have any knowledge of the allegations, accusations, rumors about Reverend Reddrick?

A: I don't think he did, sir.

Q: Okay. So, he couldn't inform the assembled congregation of anything relating to the guilt or innocence—

A: No. No, sir.

Q: All right. So, what was said beyond what he said, we're here to vote, what was said and by whom was it said to the best of your recollection?

A: The only thing that was said, Dr. Carr said he was here to vote to maintain the pastor or dismiss him. That was it.

Q: I understand that. Who else spoke, if anybody?

A: Nobody else spoke.

Q: Nobody else spoke?

A: Nobody else. Nobody else.

Q: So, this is just throw him out or keep him without any commentary on why you'd even be voting?

A: Yes. He did mention the fact why, you know, the only thing—again I'll go back and say the only thing he mentioned was that you're voting to keep the pastor or let him go.

Q: Okay. Who else spoke, if anybody?

A: That was it.

Q: So, it's 40 seconds and he says that thing you're going to vote or not vote—

A: Uh-huh.

Q: Was there any questions from the congregation?

A: There was a couple of questions.

Q: And, what were those questions if you remember?

A: I can't remember exactly what was said, but I knew there was a couple of questions asked, you know. I think—yeah, one question was asked, why are we voting, I remember that. And one of the—I can't recall who said it, but said we are voting to dismiss the pastor or retain the pastor. That was one of the questions.

Q: In the 50 year history that you have with this church, how many times has the pastor been—has there been a vote on the pastor?

A: Not in this capacity. In this situation like this, never, this is the first time.

Q: In 50 years?

A: In 50 years.

Q: And, no one questioned why the vote was being taken, something that had not been done in 50 years?

A: Un-uh.

Q: No one said, gee, why are we voting.

A: Un-uh.

Q: You told us that—

A: That one.

Q: Well, we know they were voting to dismiss or to retain. Why was the vote being taken? What was said, if anything, on why there was a vote. You didn't have a vote every week. You hadn't had a vote in 50 years like this.

A: Un-uh.

Q: Why were they told the vote was being taken?

A: To dismiss the pastor or retain the pastor.

Q: Based on what?

A: Based on the rumors that was circulating.

Q: Who mention the rumors?

A: I forget. One of the members, I can't recall who mentioned it. I can't recall.

Q: And you didn't feel that it was important in any way to mention to the people that were voting why they were voting yes or no to retain the pastor?

A: No, sir.

Q: Doesn't matter?

A: No, sir.

Q: Let's have a vote.

A: Yes, sir.

Q: Yes or no.

A: Yes, sir.

Q: Without any facts.

A: Yes, sir.

Q: Any investigation.

A: Yes, sir.

Q: Any commentary.

A: Yes, sir.

Q: Any proof.

A: Yes, sir.

Q: Just vote yes or no.

A: Yes, sir.

Q: So it's not surprising to you in the context of no information being given when people say they didn't know why they were voting yes or no.

A: No. No, sir.

Q: And in fact there are a number of people who didn't understand why they were voting and what they were voting on.

A: I would assume—not assume, I'm sorry, I take it back. I'll say, yes, there were a few of them.

Q: You know for a fact that there are a number of people—

A: A few of them.

Q: A few of them.

A: Yes, sir.

Q: Well, you know of a few, therefore, there could be many more or some more. Because you, yourself, testified here today that you didn't take any sort of scientific sample.

A: Right.

Q: so if you know of a few, meaning say, three?

A: I would say maybe five—I would say go as high as five.

Q: Five?

A: Yeah.

Q: So if there are five there could be 11 who didn't know why they were voting. Is that right?

A: I would say that. I would say no.

Q: Well, you didn't conduct a scientific sample, did you?

A: No, sir.

Q: Isn't it entirely possible the election was based upon misconceptions by some of the people who voted?

A: Uh-huh. Could have been more say voted him out, too. That's the way I look at it. Could have been more that wasn't informed that would have voted him out and could have been vice versa.

Q: So, based on a rumor you had a vote to vote in or out.

A: Yes, sir.

Q: And you think that's what a good Christian church should do.

A: Well, it's—the Baptist church, the majority, yes, sir, I would say yes, sir.

Q: And That's consistent with your constitution and your beliefs.

A: Yes, sir.

Q: Okay. Now, do you know Mrs. Holiday?

A: Mrs. Holiday, yes.

Q: Is she still around with the church?

A: Yes, she's still coming. Frances Holiday.

Q: Frances Holiday.

A: Uh-huh.

Q: She's been a longstanding member of the church, hasn't she?

A: A long time.

Q: Okay. And, are you aware that she voted to dismiss Reverend Reddrick?

A: I don't know. I have no idea, sir. I don't know, sir.

Q: Now, at the meeting, did Mrs. Holiday speak?

A: No, sir.

Q: She did not?

A: No, sir.

Q: So, she'd be wrong if she testified under oath that on January 17th at the meeting many people stated they did not know why they were there. Would she be wrong if she testified to that under oath?

A: I think she would.

Q: She'd be wrong?

A: Yes, sir.

Q: and she'd also be wrong if she said that Dean (sic) Canty said to a small group of people, you know, fornication.

A: Fornication?

Q: Fornication. In reference to why people were there to vote.

A: No, sir, I didn't.

Q: You never said that.

A: No, sir, I did not, sir. No. No.

Q: Did you talk to anybody?

A: No.

Q: Nobody.

A: No.

Q: Nobody.

A: No.

Q: Totally silent during the whole meeting?

A: At the 17th, you're still talking about the 17th?

Q: We sure are.

A: No, sir, I did not say anything.

Q: You did not talk to anybody.

A: No, sir, I did not.

Q: Okay. Do you know any reason why Mrs. Holiday would invent your having said that?

A: I don't know. I have no idea, sir.

Q: Does she have a grudge against you, too, Mr. Canty?

A: I would think we have a pretty good relationship.

Q: That's fine. Do you know any reason why she would make a false accusation that you're saying fornication?

A: No, sir. I never did say it, sir.

MR. HUME: I have nothing further at this time.

CROSS EXAMINATION

BY MR. STEPHENS:

Q: I've got one quick question. Mr. Canty, at the January 17th meeting where there was a vote held to dismiss Pastor Reddrick, did the congregation know that the purpose of that meeting was to dismiss the pastor or to retain him?

A: Yeah, they did.

Q: And, indeed the purpose of that meeting was to vote whether or not to dismiss the pastor or retain him.

A: Yeah, it was at that meeting.

Q: To the best of your knowledge, were any rumors or other accusations discussed?

A: No.

Q: So, if people think that was the purpose of the meeting, it would not be true that they weren't informed of the purpose, is that correct?

A: right, correct.

MR. STEPHENS: I have no further questions.

REDIRECT EXAMINATION

BY MR. HUME:

Q: Isn't it true that someone got up in the middle of the meeting and mentioned these rumors before they voted?

A: Not to my knowledge.

Q: Were you there for the whole meeting?

A: Yeah, I was there for the whole meeting.

Q: You're sure of that.

A: I'm positive.

Q: Okay. And there was no one who jumped up and said that there's a reason, there's an accusation—

A: One guy jumped up and said we want to know the reason, but nobody never said—accused anybody.

Q: Well, when he jumped up and said I want to know the reason, what was the response? Not telling?

A: That was the response. Nobody said anything.

Q: So you refused to inform the membership why they were voting—

A: Dr. Carr, he was conducting the meeting. He didn't know what was going on, he didn't say anything to anybody.

Q: Well, what about—were all the deacons there?

A: Yes, sir.

Q: And, when a member of your congregation demanded to know why there was a vote yes or no on the pastor, you refused to give them a reason why?

A: Yes, sir.

Q: And, by what authority do you call a meeting to make such a vote?

A: Well, the majority. Again, the majority requested it.

Q: When did the majority vote to have that meeting, sir? When was that?

A: That Sunday before the 17th.

Q: At 1:00 o'clock?

A: Yes, sir. That's when it was voted on.

Q: And there are minutes that show that?

A: Yes, sir.

Q: And what was the vote count?

A: I don't have the exact vote count.

Q: Because if the majority didn't vote to have the meeting, according to you, with your mantra of majority, majority, majority, the meeting of the 17th would be invalid, correct?

A: No, sir, I wouldn't say that. No, sir.

Q: No?

A: No.

Q: If you're saying that there has to be a majority vote of those present to have a future event take place, what proof do you have that there was in fact a majority vote on Sunday the 13th to have the meeting on Thursday the 17th?

A: I would say the majority of the church was there.

Q: What proof do you have what the vote was?

A: By hand count, but I didn't take a specific hand count, but it was by hand count.

Q: Well, how many people were in the church and how many voted yes for the meeting?

A: I couldn't say that, sir. I know there was over 100 and some people in there.

Q: Who counted them?

A: I think the secretary counted them. I can't say right off hand, sir.

Q: You're not sure.

A: I'm not sure.

Q: Are there any documents that prove that the vote for the Thursday meeting was counted?

A: You would have to check with the secretary, sir.

Q: Fine. Who's the secretary?

A: Rena Lennon.

Q: Rena Lennon, okay.

A: Yes, sir.

Q: You can rest assured we will do that.

A: Yes, sir.

Q: And if there were in fact no majority vote of those present to vote on the 13th to have a meeting on the 17th to dismiss the pastor, the meeting of the 17th would be invalid, isn't that correct?

A: No, sir.

Q: Why would it not be invalid?

A: I'm still going back to the majority vote, sir. The majority rules.

Q: If you can't prove there was a majority vote, then how do we know that the majority voted?

A: I still say the majority voted, sir.

Q: Okay, let me try this again. Mr. Canty, who counted the majority on the 13th?

A: Like I said, I have no idea who counted them, sir.

Q: So, how do you know there was a majority vote on the 13th to have the meeting on the 17th.

A: You'd have to go back to Ms. Rena Lennon and get the minutes from that meeting.

Q: Did Ms. Lennon tell you that there was in fact a counted number of people and a counted number of votes?

A: No, she did not say that.

Q: She did not say that?

A: No, sir.

Q: Then how did you know there was a valid majority vote to hold the meeting on Thursday?

A: I'm assuming there were, sir.

Q: Say again.

A: I said there were.

Q: How do you know that?

A: by the number of people there that held their hand up.

Q: Did you count them?

A: No, I did not count them.

Q: And you don't know if anyone counted them, isn't that a fact?

A: Well, somebody counted them, I'll put it that way.

Q: Do you know that of your own accord?

A: No.

Q: Do you know—

A: No, not of my own accord, no, I don't.

Q: Because obviously you'd have to count the congregation to know how many were there.

A: Uh-huh.

Q: Now, do people have to be valid members of the congregation for their vote to count?

A: Yes, sir.

Q: What makes someone a valid member of the congregation?

A: I think they asked all—they asked all the people that were not a member of the church to be excused.

Q: To be excused.

A: Right, sir.

Q: Then they counted?

A: Yes, sir.

Q: Well, you said before you didn't see them count.

A: I said they did count them, but I didn't know who took the count.

Q: Well, you heard someone counting?

A: Yes, sir.

Q: How did they count?

A: They stood up and they counted by numbers.

Q: They stood up and they counted by numbers.

A: Yes, sir.

Q: And this is on Sunday the 13th.

A: I think it was the 13th. Because that Thursday—

Q: Sunday the 13th.

A: I think it was the 13th.

Q: At about 1:00 o'clock.

A: Yes, sir. A little after one.

Q: So, someone made everyone stand up, what, like one by one like a wave in a stadium or what?

A: Right. Right.

Q: Did the individual people count their number off, or did someone out loud count that?

A: Somebody out loud counted them.

Q: Somebody out loud, counted out loud.

A: Yes, sir.

Q: And then how did people vote for the meeting on Thursday? Did they raise their hands?

A: Right, they did.

Q: Raised hands. And did someone count the raised hands?

A: Yeah, they did.

Q: And, who counted the raised hands?

A: I don't—like I said, I don't know who counted them.

Q: But you heard them count out loud.

A: right.

Q: Someone counted out loud.

A: Yeah, somebody did.

Q: And, could that be heard throughout the whole congregation?

A: Right, it did.

Q: Everyone would hear that?

A: Right.

MR. HUME: I have nothing further at this time.

MR. STEPHENS: That's it.

(WHEREUPON THE TAKING OF THE DEPOSITION WAS CONCLUDED)

In the thirty-second chapter of the Book of Exodus, Moses leaves Aaron in charge of the people, while he goes up the mountain to consult God. While he's there, they violate the covenant made between them and God. When it became known, Moses interceded with God to save them from God's wrath. But when he, Moses, returned to the camp, this is what happened:

And when Moses saw that the people had broken loose, for Aaron had let them break loose, to their shame among their enemies, then Moses stood in the gate of the camp, and said, 'Who is on the Lord's side? Come to me.' And all the sons of Levi gathered themselves together to him. And he said to them, 'Thus says the Lord God of Israel, put every man his sword on his side, and go to and from gate to gate throughout the camp, and slay every man his brother, and every man his companion, and every man his neighbor.' And the sons of Levi did according to the word of Moses; and there fell of the people that day about three thousand men. And Moses said, 'Today you have ordained yourselves for the service of the Lord, each one at the cost of his son and of his brother, that he may bestow a blessing upon you this day.' (vss. 25-29)

Likewise, Jesus said, in Matthew the eighteenth chapter and the sixth verse, "But whoever causes one of these little ones who believe in me to sin, it would be better for him to have a great millstone fastened round his neck and to be drowned in the depth of the sea" (The New Oxford, Annotated Bible).

Indeed, both Moses and Jesus made it clear, that there are severe consequences for anyone who misleads the people of God. As I watched those two deacons that day being deposed, as they wiggled and squirmed like worms in hot grease, I wondered if they realized the magnitude of their sin. Furthermore, I wondered how these aged men could so blatantly lie, with no apparent signs of being ashamed.

Yet, as strange as it may seem, as I listened to them shamefully trying to distance themselves from their sin, I did take much comfort from the fact that both of them have nieces that are among my staunchest supporters. Like the Levites, these supporters ordained themselves to the service of God at the cost of their own family and like the Levites, God will bestow a blessing upon them. Seldom in life is one so privileged to be the beneficiary of such courageous faith. For that alone, I feel extremely blessed.

Now worship at The Village continued. And what started out as just a temporary place to meet until the lawsuit was settled had now turned into something unexpected. Some in the group started telling me that they did not want to go back even if we won the lawsuit. They started explaining to me and to each other in our occasional group meetings that something special had happened to them. They were no longer grieving. They were no longer being swallowed by bitterness. They were no longer home sick for the place they left. They said that they were even glad that they were no longer there. They felt that they had arrived at a spiritual place that was better than the place they were before and felt blessed by the suffering and sacrifice that they'd made. One woman even said that she was glad that God allowed it to happen.

As I listened to the people describe their transformation, I knew it was genuine because it was happening to me also. I too was being lifted—lifted to a place above my pain, above my sorrow and above my grief. I felt the joy of God again. I felt reinvigorated, enlightened, as never before. I felt as if I'd been resurrected.

And despite the fact that the slander was still unresolved and even without any promotion or fanfare, others still joined. When asked what was the most single thing they liked about The Village, the members and visitors would all say the love that the people had for one another. To me, this was a confirmation of the power of true worship—the worship of God in spirit and in truth.

Moreover, the progress of The Village Academy was another source of inspiration to the people and to myself. We finally got the 501(c)3 approval from the Internal Revenue. The Academy was now an official non-profit organization with unlimited potential.

Another source of comfort to me was the local chapter of the NAMI (National Alliance on Mental Illness) organization. I joined it and found support and advice from others whose lives had also been affected by family members with mental illnesses of various kinds. My affiliation there in addition to the support and advice, eliminated my sense of isolation as well. Another source of my optimism was a gift given to me and to The Village Academy by my son and his wife. It was their old computer which was in excellent condition. With it, I started writing this manuscript. All of this was accomplished now as the year came to an end.

The New Year began with great anticipation. Although the relationship between my wife and me was still in a coma, I continued to pray for a miracle. But instead of a miracle, I got another set of separation papers. This time when I got the papers, I decided to leave our home and not wait for a judge to order me to do so. Nevertheless, right on the heels of that set back came some good news. My lawyer called and told me that we finally got a trial date.

CHAPTER 6

The Judge's Ruling

The day of my long awaited trial finally came. Two years and one month had been spent compiling the evidence that would have cleared my name. Since I didn't get a church trial, it was my hope that the civil courts would be the place where I would be vindicated. The evidence clearly showed that the church had bylaws and they were violated in my termination.

However, the one factor that continued to trouble me deeply was the fact that Judge Carroll would be the judge presiding. Judges have wide discretionary power and their biases can and do affect their rulings. There was no doubt in my mind but that Judge Carroll had a bias toward me and that he was going to find a way in the law to see that I never returned to that church.

I wanted a trial to clear my name and to expose the wrong that was done to me by the deacons. A trial and a favorable ruling based on the overwhelming evidence would have done just that. The spirit never revealed to me that I would be going back to Mount Calvary. I had no desire to do so, but I did want the truth to be known. Only a trial could do that. Whether a revote would be ordered or a reinstatement, I would have the opportunity to resign but with my reputation restored.

My rationale for believing that Judge Carroll would be bias was a situation that occurred in 1997. It involved the case where three members had been expelled from the church. Every effort had been made to reconcile them with the church but to no avail. When the church voted to allow women to preach, it was a cause of some controversy.

A long debate and discussion of it by the members took place prior to the vote of the church. The decision was to allow women to preach. But in spite of the vote, one member in particular, a lady who had already been expelled but was allowed to remain in hopes that she would eventually reconcile, took advantage of that controversy and tried to mount an uprising in the church. It was then that the deacons and I decided that there was no choice but to enforce what the church had already voted to do sometime ago.

Every procedure governing that process was meticulously followed as depicted in the Hiscox Guide. Although it was a cause of much pain for me at the time, I was convinced that her wrongdoing should be confronted but in the spirit of love. However, the expelled parties decided to challenge the decision of the church by filing a lawsuit. Judge Carroll was the judge in the case. In the preliminary hearing, he ordered that they be allowed to return to the church for thirty days and then ordered the church to revote to see if it would restore their membership. The vote would be done under the supervision of a neutral moderator.

That was done and the original decision made by the church was upheld. When the matter returned before the judge, he was still reluctant to rule according to the law but the attorney representing the church at that time, confronted him and told him that he had no choice in the matter. After the trial, I felt that Judge Carroll condemned me for the violation of some unwritten rule.

I knew that expulsion of a church member is a violation of a powerful custom in our community. No member is ever expelled from our churches no matter how wrong their conduct. If anyone has to leave, it's always the pastor. And if he confronts the sin in the church, even in the spirit of love and if he refuses to submit to the powers that be and even if he has broad support in the church, he's going to be called a dictator and troublemaker by some. Yet that action, as extreme as it was, did bring peace in the church. For five years afterwards the church continued to grow and prosper, financially, spiritually and numerically. That growth and prosperity culminated in the building of a new sanctuary that was ninety percent finished when this incident involving my family occurred.

Now five years later, as I appeared before him again—but this time as a victim in a preliminary hearing—his scorn for me was verified. I heard him angrily make this statement in regards to me, "Whatever happened to that nice lady he put out of the church?" In his mind I was a threat to the law and order on the plantation. He and the trusted servants had decided now that it was time for me to leave. Although I told both attorneys who represented me about the judge's bias, neither one of them felt that it would interfere with his ruling: but I knew better.

That's the history surrounding Judge Carroll and me as I once again found myself in his courtroom. When the court was called to order, the church attorney made a motion for dismissal. He offered several cases to support his position. After a brief argument on the merits of the motion, the judge summoned the two attorneys to his chamber. I knew then that I was not going to get a trial. Vicious dogs are often given a hearing to determine the validity of any charges against them, but as for me, I would not even be afforded the rights of a dog.

When my own attorney confirmed to me what I already knew, although disappointed, it was nevertheless a further confirmation of what the spirit had already revealed to me. But in order to add insult to injury they, the church, was *willing* to offer me a letter stating that none of this had anything to do with a rumor and furthermore, they would commend me for my outstanding service of the past fourteen years. They would state that the action they took was for the protection of the church. I told my attorney that my conscience would not allow me to agree to a lie. I told him to go back and tell the judge to rule what he's going to rule but I would rely on God to now clear my name.

The judge ruled that since I did not have a contract, even though the church had bylaws that specified the terms of the pastor's termination, the church was not legally obligated to abide by them because I was an at will employee with no protection under the bylaws. On the basis of that technicality, once again I was denied due process. When he finished announcing his ruling, some of the members applauded. And I wondered if they knew what they were doing. My wife was there and would have had to testify. I took some comfort in the fact that at least she would be spared that shame.

Meanwhile, as I went back to The Village, accompanied by friends and supporters, I thought of the unpleasant fact that I would have to continue living with that sordid slander, unless God himself removed it. Suddenly like a knock on a door, these words of the apostle Paul visited my soul:

> And to keep me from being too elated by the abundance of revelations, a thorn was given me in the flesh, a messenger of Satan, to harass me, to keep me from being too elated. Three times I besought the lord about this, that it should leave me; but he said to me, 'My grace is sufficient for you, for my power is made perfect in weakness.' For the sake of Christ, then, I am content with weaknesses that the power of Christ may rest upon me. For the sake of Christ, then, I am content with weaknesses, insults, hardships, persecutions, and calamities; for when I am weak, then I am strong. (2nd Corinthians, 12th chapter, verses 7-10, The New Oxford Annotated Bible)

That was my soul's consolation now. I didn't have my reputation back but I did have God's grace, the enjoyment of his favor. I left the courtroom determined, with the help of God, to turn my negative into a positive. Instead of running from this slander, I would embrace it and use it for the glory of God.

For I was convinced now that God had made me weak, in order for his strength to be manifested in my life. Back at The Village, the first question to me was, "How do you feel?" My answer was that I felt relieved. I asked those who were there if they wanted to go on? They all said, "Yes."

My oldest brother was there. My youngest brother drove from Philadelphia to be with me. Dr. Thurman Everett was there, along with other blessed supporters who had stood with me throughout this whole ordeal. They each left us with words of encouragement and inspiration. Then Dr. Everett took up a love offering. The Spirit of God lifted our hearts and the events of the morning officially launched the beginning of The Village Ministry.

CHAPTER 7

The Conclusion

While writing the introduction to the book, a friend of mine was visiting me in my study. By coincidence, I just happened to ask him if he had any material on the subject of lynching. He said—to my surprise—as a matter of fact, he did. He immediately got up, went outside to his car, came back and handed me this article.

Washington's most progressive Black Newspaper

How to keep a Black Man Down

From one White slave owner to another

In the words of Willie Lynch in 1712, the man for whom Lynchburg, Virginia was named, there are many ways in which you can keep control over your slave.
His wisdom of 282 years has not changed.

Gentlemen:

I greet you here on the bank of the James River in the year of our lord, one thousand seven hundred and twelve. First, I shall thank you, the gentlemen of the Colony of Virginia, for bringing me here. I am here to help you solve some of your problems with slaves. Your invitation reached me on my modest plantation in the West Indies where I have experimented with some of the newest and still the oldest methods for control of slaves.

Ancient Rome would envy us if my program is implemented. As our boat sailed south on the James River, named for our illustrious King James, whose Bible we cherish, I saw enough to know that your problem is not unique. While Rome used cords of wood and crosses for standing human bodies along the old highways in great number, you are here using the tree and the rope on occasion.

I caught the whiff of a dead slave hanging from a tree a couple of miles back. You are not only losing valuable stock by hangings, you are having uprisings, slaves are running away, your crops are sometimes left in the fields too long for maximum profit, you suffer occasional fires, your animals are killed, gentlemen. You know what your problems are: I do not need to elaborate. I am not here to enumerate your problems, I am here to introduce you to a method of solving them.

In my bag here, I have a fool-proof method for controlling your Black slaves. I guarantee everyone of you that if installed correctly it will control the slaves for at least 300 years. My method is simple, any member of your family or any overseer can use it.

I have outlined a number of differences among the slaves, and I take these differences and make them bigger. I use fear, distrust and envy for control purposes. These methods have worked on my modest plantation in the West Indies, and it will work throughout the south.

Take this simple little list of differences and think about them. On the top of my list is "Age" but it is there because it only starts with an "A"; the second is "Color" or shade; there is intelligence, size of plantations, attitudes of owners, whether the slaves live in the valley, on a hill, East, West North, South, have fine, or coarse hair, or is tall or short.

Now that you have a list of differences, I shall give you an outline of action—but before that, I shall assure you that distrust is stronger than trust, and envy is stronger than adulation, respect or admiration. The Black Slave, after receiving this indoctrination, shall carry on and will become self refueling and self generating for hundreds of years, maybe thousands.

Don't forget, you must pitch the old Black vs. the Young Black male, and the young Black male vs. the old Black male. You must use the dark skin slaves vs. the light skin slaves; and light skin slaves vs. the dark skin slaves. You must use the female vs. the male, and the male, vs. the female.

You must also have your servants and overseers distrust all Blacks, but it is necessary that your slaves trust and depend on us. They must love, respect and trust only us. Gentlemen, these kits are your keys to control, use them. Have your wives and children use them. Never miss opportunity. My plan is guaranteed, and the good thing about this plan is that if used intensely for one year, the slaves themselves will remain perpetually distrustful.

When I finished reading the article, I knew it was important. But I didn't see how I could use it in my introduction. However, several days later, like a sudden landing of a beautiful butterfly on a garden flower, this thought landed in my mind. The cause of my personal tragedy had its roots grounded in the Lynch doctrine. Then that thought expanded to this one. Not only does my personal tragedy have its roots there, but also the collective tragedy of my whole race, the African American people. What was handed to me was the blue print developed by the slave holding aristocracy of America, to control, and perpetuate the psychological slavery of African American people.

The continuing manifestation of this spiritual illness can be seen, I believe, in what Dr. Cornell West calls, "the nihilism that increasingly pervades black communities." He defines nihilism "as the lived experience of coping with a life of horrifying meaninglessness, hopelessness, and (most important) lovelessness." According to Dr. West, "The frightening result is a numbing detachment from others, the world." Furthermore, he continues "life without meaning, hope, and love breeds a cold hearted, mean-spirited outlook that destroys both the individual and others" (Race Matters, Dr. Cornell West, pp. 22-23).

What other explanation exist for the wide spread self-mutilation that exist among us? What other explanation exist for the continuing self hate endemic among us? That the condition of the nihilistic threat has grown more powerful now than ever before, Dr. West advances two reasons, "the saturation of market forces and market moralities in black life and the present crisis in black leadership" (p.24).

I agree wholeheartedly with his analysis, but I would like to add one more reason to the list. Idolatry is in too many of the churches in America including the African American churches. The words of God spoken by the eighteenth century prophet Amos still rings true:

> I hate, I despise your feasts, and I take no delight in your solemn assemblies. Even though you offer me your burnt offerings and cereal offerings, I will not accept them, and the peace offerings of your fatted beasts, I will not look upon. Take away from me the noise of your songs; to the melody of your harps I will not listen. But let justice roll down like waters, and righteousness like an ever-flowing stream." (The book of Amos, chapter 5, verses 21-24, The New Oxford Annotated Bible)

Indeed, I believe that the Jesus that is talked about in too many of the churches in America today is not the Jesus of scripture, nor is he the one that God raised from the dead, but a dead idol created by men to give legitimacy to their corrupt traditions, customs and practices. What other explanation is there for the continuing psychological slavery of the African American people in these churches? What other explanation is there for the cold heartedness and lack of love even among church people. Naturally there are many exceptions and I thank God for them. But the truth of the matter is that the institutional church in America is not setting the people free from the Lynch doctrine but in many ways through its perverted traditions, customs and practices are agents for perpetuating it.

Furthermore, the Spirit has shown me that there are comparisons with my wife's mental state of mind and the collective mental state of mind of America. Just as I am a victim of my wife's delusional thinking, paranoia, and schizophrenia, the whole race of African American people are victims of America's collective state of mental illness. What other valid explanation is there for their collective fear, demonstrated by their love affair with guns? What other valid explanation can one offer for the excessive spending for national defense, year after year? What other valid explanation is there for the brutal enslaving of a race of people for hundreds of years and then blaming them for it, while at the same time, defaming them and hating them and then denying any responsibility for their wounds.

And, given the fact now that this nation is the world's only military super power, I believe that she will become a threat to the stability of the family of nations of the world if not treated or converted. And just as I love my wife, I love America. But I don't love America's sickness or her sins.

In view of this dire assessment, the next logical question is—Is there hope? Is there any hope that the African American people can be collectively delivered from the psychological slavery perpetuated by the Lynch doctrine? Again, I agree with Dr. West, "nihilism is not overcome by arguments or analyses; it is tamed by love and care. Any disease of the soul must be conquered by a turning of one's soul. This turning is done through one's own affirmation of one's worth—an affirmation fueled by the concern of others." Dr. West says this love ethic, "has nothing to do with sentimental feelings or tribal connections. Rather it is a last attempt at generating a sense of agency among a downtrodden people." Furthermore, he says, "self love and love of others are both modes toward increasing self-valuation and encouraging political resistance in one's community. These modes of valuation and resistance," according to Dr. West, "are rooted in a subversive memory—the best of one's past without romantic nostalgia—and guided by a universal love ethic." This "love ethic" he says, "must be at the center of" what he calls, "the politics of conversion" (p.29). In the Thorndike Barnhart Advanced Dictionary, one simple definition of the word politics, is this, "wise in looking out for one's own interest." I like that definition. For wisdom rooted in God is priceless. The First and Great Commandment is to love God, to love our neighbor, as *we love ourself.*

Finally, says Dr. West "The advocates of a politics of conversion never lose sight of the structural conditions that shape the sufferings and lives of people. Yet, unlike liberal structuralists, the advocates of a politics of conversion meet the nihilistic threat head on." Similarly, he affirms, "Like conservative behaviorism, the politics of conversion openly confronts the self-destructive and inhumane actions of black people."

He concludes, "Unlike conservative behaviorists, the politics of conversion situates these actions within inhumane circumstances [but does not thereby exonerate them]" (Race Matters, Dr. Cornell West, pp. 30-31).

That's the goal of The Village Worship Center and the Academy, to liberate the minds of its members and students from the psychological slavery of the Lynch doctrine through what Dr West calls the politics of conversion, which is grounded in the love of God, self and others. That such a conversion is possible is made clear by the apostle Paul who said "Do not conform to this world but be ye transformed by the renewing of your mind, that you may prove what is the will of God, what is good and acceptable and perfect" (12th chapter of Roman's, verse 2).

Just as the collective mind set of the African American people has been conditioned to conform to the Lynch doctrine for the purpose of serving the interest of their oppressor, their minds can also be renewed to serve wisely their own interest and the interest of God and his kingdom.

Consequently, I believe that should be the goal of every religious institution in the African American community. I also believe that each one of these institutions should have an enrichment school dedicated to the same purpose. In the process of doing that, we must keep in mind that the mode and means of accomplishing the goal, cannot be sorely transplanted from other people's experiences only but they must be uniquely applicable to our own. Additionally, the success and relevance of those institutions should be measured by the degree to which the goal is being realized in the lives of the people.

In my view, any institution in our community not dedicated to that purpose, is unholy, irrelevant and unworthy of the people's support.

With a renewed collective mind deeply rooted in the universal love ethics of self-love and love of others, we can reclaim our sons and daughters from the plantation of the prison system in America and restore them as viable members of our community. In addition, we could operate and own more businesses in our communities, which would allow us to employ more of our own people. I could go on and on with many more examples of the positive changes that would sprout from the ground of self love and love of others.

This same goal of deliverance is the goal of Jesus, enshrined in the following words:

> The Spirit of the Lord is upon me, because he has anointed me to preach good news to the poor. He has sent me to proclaim release to the captives and recovering of sight to the blind, to set at liberty those who are oppressed, to proclaim the acceptable year of the Lord." (St. Luke the fourth chapter verse 18-19, The New Oxford Annotated Bible)

And yes America, there is a word from the Lord to you as well. You can take a giant step toward good collective mental health by acknowledging the wrong you've done to the Native American people and the African American people. Confirm the validity of the reconciliation by offering them a reparation package. If we fail in our duty, our conscience will condemn us, and God will judge us.

BIBLIOGRAPHY

Wolfgang, Marvin e. The World Book Encyclopedia
L. Volume 12, Field Enterprises Educational
Corporation, 1975.

Hiscox, Edward T. Principles and Practices for Baptist Churches
Kregel Publlications, Grand Rapids, MI

The New Oxford Annotated Bible
Oxford University Press, 1962.

West, Cornel. Race Matters
Vintage Books, A Division of Random House, Inc.
New York, 1994.

Thorndike, Barnhart. Advanced Dictionary
Second Edition
Scot, Foresman and Company,
Glenview, Illinois. 1974.

ABOUT THE AUTHOR

Author and publisher, C H. Reddrick, is a 1967 graduate of Fayetteville State University. He attended Shaw University Seminary, Raleigh, North Carolina In 1978 he graduated from South eastern Baptist Theological Seminary, Wake Forest, North Carolina where he received a Masters of Divinty degree. He is also a Vietnam War veteran. Pastor Reddrick has pastored in Virginia and North Carolina for over twenty years.

He lives in Wilmington, North Carolina and now pastors The Village Worship Center.

Contact Information:

Phone (910) 762-9387
(910) 612-5120

Edwards Brothers,Inc!
Thorofare, NJ 08086
22 March, 2011
BA2011081